ADVANCEDARPEGGIO
SOLOINGFORGUITAR

Creative Arpeggio Studies for Modern Rock & Fusion Guitar

CHRISBROOKS

FUNDAMENTALCHANGES

Advanced Arpeggio Soloing for Guitar

An In-Depth Guide to Arpeggios for Modern Rock and Fusion Guitar

ISBN: 978-1-78933-028-1

Published by www.fundamental-changes.com

www.fundamental-changes.com

Twitter: **@guitar_joseph**

Over 10,000 fans on Facebook: **FundamentalChangesInGuitar**

Facebook: ChrisBrooksGuitar

Instagram: **Fundamental Changes**

Instagram: chrisbrooksguitarist

For over 350 Free Guitar Lessons with Videos Check Out

www.fundamental-changes.com

Cover Image Copyright Shutterstock: Roman Voloshyn

Contents

Introduction

Since writing my last book, *Sweep Picking Speed Strategies for Guitar,* I've been very keen to complete the book you're reading now. Knowing that technique is only as valuable as what you use it for, I've been excitedly compiling this volume of vocabulary-based concepts to cover the next steps in arpeggio playing.

As a younger player, I was inspired by the wave of technical rock players in the 1980s and wanted to learn those chops for myself. On the flip side, I was becoming more aware of how *hip* jazz and fusion players could sound through their note choices and phrasing ideas. Thankfully, the two are not mutually exclusive, and my goal ever since has been to draw inspiration from many corners into my playing.

Throughout this book, you will accumulate an arsenal of ideas that will work equally well over rock, metal, jazz and fusion vamps. From triad pairing through to voicing approaches, phrasing concepts, sequences, and connecting scales to arpeggios, this book aims to deliver new revelations each time you read it.

Many of the concepts come with some theoretical background, but you needn't be a jazz major to benefit from the licks. Theory, from my perspective, is not a set of rules, but a collection of observations regarding why some things work and others might not. Accumulating this information as you go is useful for applying good ideas to as many situations as you can imagine, while avoiding sounds you dislike.

This material can be absorbed on three levels, from superficial to fully-utilised, depending on your experience:

Level One: Learn the licks as written and use them over the suggested chords

Level Two: Understand the motivation behind each lick

Level Three: Be able to apply the theory behind the lick to other arpeggios, keys or modes

Each chapter concludes with a short list of goals. Unlike my previous books, this one can be approached in a modular way, allowing you to jump back and forth between chapters if some concepts inspire you more than others. Advanced players might like to cherry-pick all their favourite ideas, while intermediate players will benefit from studying the material in sequence.

Since a great deal of this book is dedicated to adding creative sounds to your arpeggio playing, listening to the audio tracks will be extremely beneficial to expand your musical palette. Each example is played at two speeds. The backing is also repeated with the lead parts muted to give you an opportunity to play the licks over the same harmony. You'll also find one-chord vamps of the most important chord types, so you can really stretch out with improvisation, combining multiple ideas over the tracks to create some great music.

Enjoy the topics ahead and best of luck being creative in your solos!

Chris Brooks

Get the Audio

The audio files for this book are available to download for free from **www.fundamental-changes.com.** The link is in the top right-hand corner. Just select this book title from the drop-down menu and follow the instructions to get the audio.

We recommend that you download the files directly to your computer, not to your tablet, and extract them there before adding them to your media library. You can then put them on your tablet, iPod or burn them to CD. On the download page there is a help PDF and we also provide technical support via the contact form.

For over 350 Free Guitar Lessons with Videos Check out:

www.fundamental-changes.com

Twitter: **@guitar_joseph**

Over 10,000 fans on Facebook: **FundamentalChangesInGuitar**

Instagram: **FundamentalChanges**

A (Little) Bit of Background Music Theory

Although practical application is the primary motivation of this book, some background information will make it easier to use this material in real-life playing situations. The following breakdown will ensure you understand the terms I'll be using and how they relate to the music we'll be looking at.

If you've studied my previous book, *Sweep Picking Speed Strategies for Guitar* and also have some experience playing scales and modes, you're already set to work through the material in this book. Feel free to jump right into Chapter One.

Many of the examples are written in the key of G Major using triads, arpeggios and modes from this key.

The key of G contains the notes,

G (root),

A (major 2nd)

B (major 3rd)

C (perfect 4th)

D (perfect 5th)

E (major 6th)

F# (major 7th)

Numerically, the major scale has the simple *formula* 1 2 3 4 5 6 7, because it's the scale we most often compare other scales to in Western music.

The "spellings" of other modes and arpeggios reference this numbering system, with any applicable sharps or flats added. For example, the Lydian mode has the formula 1 2 3 #4 5 6 7, as it is identical to the major scale in every way with the exception of the fourth note being raised by a semitone.

Triads and 7ths in the key of G Major

In the key of G Major, the triads and seventh chords are:

I.   *G Major* – G, B, D (1, 3, 5) and *G Major Seventh* – G, B, D, F# (1, 3, 5, 7)

II. *A Minor* – A, C, E (1, b3, 5) and *A Minor Seventh* – A, C, E, G (1, b3, 5, b7)

III. *B Minor* – B, D, F# (1, b3, 5) and *B Minor Seventh* – B, D, F#, A (1, b3, 5, b7)

IV. *C Major* – C, E, G (1, 3, 5) and *C Major Seventh* – C, E, G, B (1, 3, 5, 7)

V.   *D Major* – D, F#, A (1, 3, 5) and *D Dominant Seventh* – D, F#, A, C (1, 3, 5, b7)

VI. *E Minor* – E, G, B (1, b3, 5) and *E Minor Seventh* – E, G, B, D (1, b3, 5, b7)

VII. *F# Diminished* – F#, A, C (1, b3, b5) and *F# Minor Seventh (flat five)* or *Half-Diminished* – F#, A, C, E (1, b3, b5, b7)

Making each chord the focus or *tonal centre* of a rhythm vamp is the gateway to playing *modes*.

Modes in the key of G Major

Most intermediate players are familiar with how a major scale and its relative minor scale create two sounds using the same key signature. The concept of *modes* is an expansion of this idea, whereby every degree of the scale and its matching chord can be treated as a new tonal centre. By splitting the key into seven portions – one per scale degree – modal flavours are created.

Think of the seven modes as siblings with overlapping DNA, yet distinct individual personalities.

You might already know the two most common modes in Western music: *Ionian* (aka, the major scale) and *Aeolian* (the natural minor scale). Modes associated with major chords (i.e. their first chord is a major chord) are considered *major modes* and those associated with minor (or diminished) chords (i.e. their first chord is a minor chord) are *minor modes*.

The seven modes of G Major and their numeric representations are:

1. *G Ionian* (the major scale) – 1, 2, 3, 4, 5, 6, 7 or G, A, B, C, D, E, F#

2. *A Dorian* (minor mode with a major 6th) – 1, 2, b3, 4, 5, 6, b7 or A, B, C, D, E, F#, G

3. *B Phrygian* (minor mode with a minor 2nd) – 1, b2, b3, 4, 5, b6, b7 or B, C, D, E, F#, G, A

4. *C Lydian* (major mode with an augmented 4th) – 1, 2, 3, #4, 5, 6, 7 or C, D, E, F#, G, A, B

5. *D Mixolydian* (major mode with a minor 7th) – 1, 2, 3, 4, 5, 6, b7 or D, E, F#, G, A, B, C

6. *E Aeolian* (the natural minor scale) – 1, 2, b3, 4, 5, b6, b7 or E, F#, G, A, B, C, D

7. *F# Locrian* (minor mode with a minor 2nd and diminished 5th) – 1, 2, b3, 4, b5, b6, b7 or F#, G, A, B, C, D, E

Other modes and scales referred to in this book will be broken down as they relate to the examples at hand. For extra reading on scales and modes, check out *Guitar Scales in Context* by Joseph Alexander, and *Rock Guitar Mode Mastery* by Chris Zoupa. Both are published by Fundamental Changes.

In the first two chapters of this book, you will get a sense of how simple it can be to create modal sounds by combining different arpeggios over static chords to expand the palette of colours available beyond the basic chord tones.

Sweep Picking and Picking Orientation

Sweep picking plays a big role in fast, economical arpeggio playing. Many of the pick strokes in the examples are optimised for the systems laid out in my book *Sweep Picking Speed Strategies for Guitar*, so please refer to that for the ultimate guide to sweep picking development and mastery.

Ascending sweep picking is performed with a *downward pick slant* and descending sweeping is done with an *upward pick slant*, just as you would angle the pick while strumming to create a smooth motion from string to string.

When changing directions, string changes are handled with a mix of picking around the strings (*outside picking*) or between them (*inside picking*). To avoid getting the pick trapped between strings when turning arpeggios around, refer to the notes on *upscaping* and *downscaping* in my previous book.

Every pick stroke is included in every lick within this book, so you'll never have to guess how I play them. You can experiment with other string-changing strategies. Where relevant, some alternatives to the assigned pick strokes are mentioned.

Chapter One: Get Snazzy with Triad Pairs

I first heard what turned out to be a *triad pair* in Cher's 1987 hit, *I've Found Someone*. Played on a layered piano and synth pad sound, the catchy intro keyboard hook alternated between two triads and inversions with the right hand while holding a static bass note with the left. What I picked up from that little hook is that you can combine stationary and moving ideas to create something uniquely melodic.

In modern Jazz and Fusion, triad pairing is a common melodic device used by improvisers. However, Rock guitar players can get in on the fun too, since triad pairs are a perfect fit for sweep picking and other techniques while broadening the capabilities of the humble triad.

A triad pair is merely the alternating of two triads within a phrase. Pairs are commonly (but not limited to) neighbouring triads within a key and can use various cluster sizes and directions. By combining the tones of two adjacent triads, six notes are at your disposal to create melodies that outline different modes, build tension and release, imply upper chord extensions and create some unique *outside playing* concepts.

You can try any triad pair over any chord as you experiment, but for the best results, take care with pairs that clash with chord tones. For example, triad pairs containing the note C will sound pretty awful against the B note of a G chord. In this chapter, I'll focus on triad pairs that sound great and show you how to push the boundaries without creating dissonance.

Whether you're a rocker or a jazz-head, there will be triad pairs that suit your style. The information in this chapter is thorough, but even a passing glance will turn you into the thinking man's arpeggio player.

Major Triad Pairs

One of the most common triad pairs contains triads built on the IV and V chord of the major key, for example C Major and D Major in the key of G.

Before getting into the sounds, let's look at a simple way to map out triad pairs.

These fretboard diagrams use three strings at a time to locate C Major (black markers) and D Major triad (white markers). You can find various triad shapes in these fretboard diagrams by approaching the three-string groups from all angles, using different combinations of one note and two notes per string.

C and D triad pairs on the 6th, 5th and 4th strings

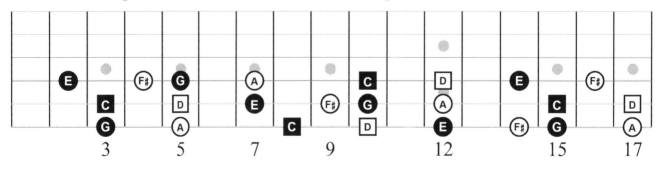

C and D triad pairs on the 5th, 4th and 3rd strings

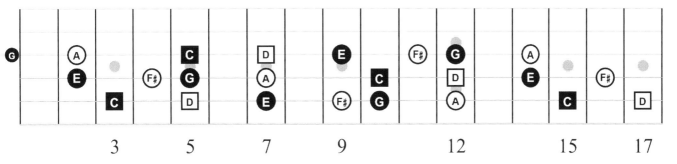

C and D triad pairs on the 4th, 3rd and 2nd strings

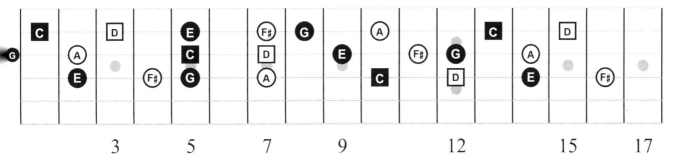

C and D triad pairs on the 3rd, 2nd and 1st strings

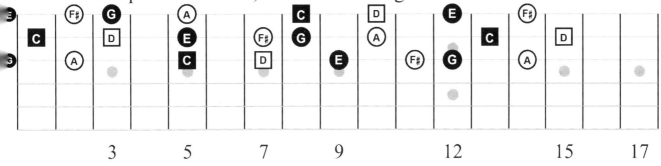

When playing triad pairs over rhythm parts, pay attention to the notes that *don't* belong to each underlying chord, because these are the *colour tones* that determine how well a triad pair suits the chord underneath.

is most common to apply the IV/V chords over the II, IV and V chords of a key.

ver a C chord in the key of G, the C/D triad pair creates a *Lydian* sound, since the combined notes spell out e 1, 2, 3, #4, 5, 6 degrees of C Lydian. The C triad contains the notes 1, 3 and 5, and the D triad contains the th, #11th and 13th (2, #4 and 6) extensions of the C chord.

hen played over a D chord, the C and D triads imply a modal sound of D Mixolydian (1 2 3 4 5 6 b7), with x of the mode's degrees contained. The C triad contains the b7, 9(2) and 11(4) and the D triad contains the 1, and 5. The 4th (11th) is said to clash with the 3rd of the D triad, but weaving in and out of triad pairs doesn't eate the same dissonance that a long melody note might.

ver an A Minor chord, the C/D triad pair spells out the *Dorian* tonality with the degrees 1, b3, 4, 5, 6 and b7 A Dorian represented.

Let's use the three-string format of these triads as a starting point for some practical work.

Example 1a uses D and C triads over a C chord. Each four-note unit begins with an upstroke to take advantage of a downward sweep from the A to the G string. You can repeat this form using any of the three-string groups.

Maintain a downward pick slant throughout this exercise and use your fretting hand index finger for each of the position shifts.

Example 1a:

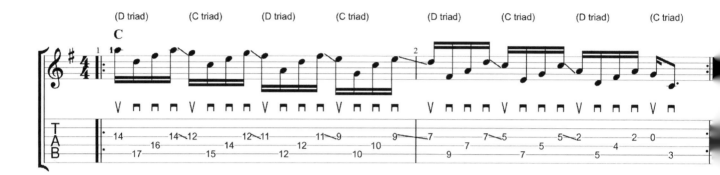

When playing only a C Major triad fragment over the chord (as shown in Example 1b), the Lydian sound is lost since there is nothing to identify the C chord underneath as a I, IV or V chord.

Example 1b:

Using the same shapes as Example 1a (this time over a D chord), Example 1c is played in quintuplet groups. You can develop a feel for tuplets like these by playing the entire phrase evenly without regard for which notes fall on beats, then practise *rushing* each shape, so that the first of each group of five lands on a beat. Introduce the metronome only after you've followed the previous steps.

Example 1c:

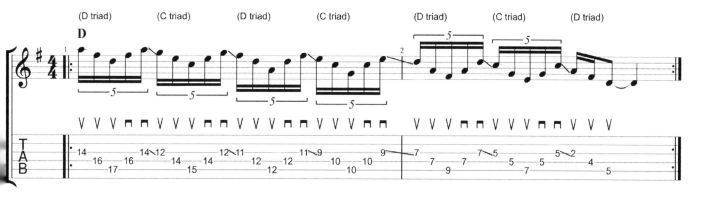

Now let's explore the Dorian tonality by using IV and V triads over the II (minor) chord.

Example 1d demonstrates how to connect different three-string groups, rather than moving horizontally along the neck. Triad pairs are used on string groups one, two and three, as well as strings four, five and six.

On the remaining three-string groups, only one sliding pair is used on each. By learning the shapes that exist on all string groups, you'll be free to move vertically and horizontally wherever you choose.

Example 1d:

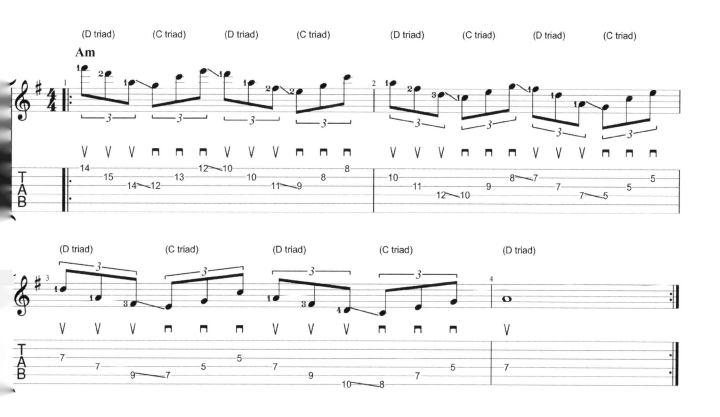

Triads in each pair don't have to be used in equal measure or always alternate on downbeats. Example 1e begins with four notes of a D triad, then three notes of a C triad. Cycling these seven 1/16th notes creates a polyrhythmic melodic feel. At the end of the lick, just three notes of the D triad and two of the C triad are used to avoid predictability.

Example 1e:

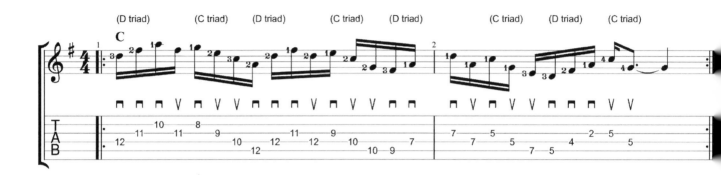

Defying expectation can be done in smaller ways too. By using four strings for each triad, bar one of Example 1f weaves in and out of equal portions of C and D triads, but tips the balance in favour of the C triad with nine out of fourteen notes in bar two.

Each note on the D string is fretted with the third finger, which will also handle the rolling in bar one, beats and 2.

Example 1f:

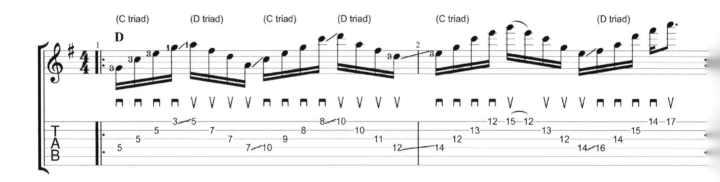

With the sweep picking *Speed Shapes* from my previous book, *Sweep Picking Speed Strategies for Guitar*, triad pairs can be created with larger forms too.

C Major Speed Shape 1   C Major Speed Shape 2

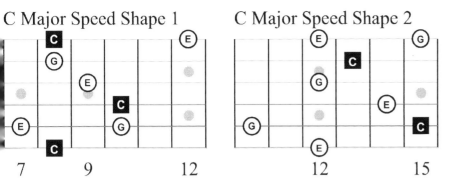

Example 1g uses the lowest shape of the C triad, the highest shape of the D triad, and bridges the gap with two middle shapes in between.

Example 1g:

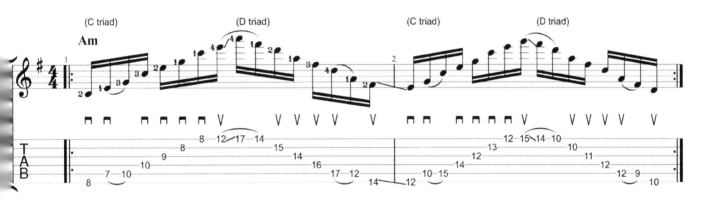

Minor Triad Pairs

Neighbouring minor triads like the II and III chords of the major scale make another popular triad pair that's utilised by many contemporary Jazz and Fusion improvisers.

In the key of G Major, the adjacent minor triads are A Minor and B Minor, and are mapped out as follows:

Am and Bm triad pairs on the 6th, 5th and 4th strings

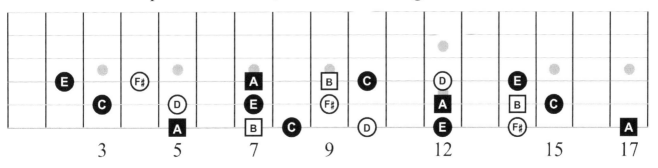

Am and Bm triad pairs on the 5th, 4th and 3rd strings

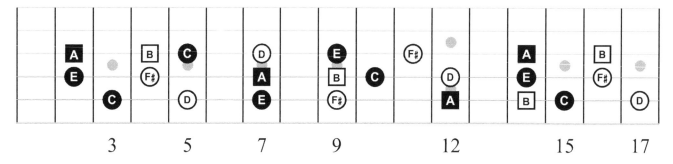

Am and Bm triad pairs on the 4th, 3rd and 2nd strings

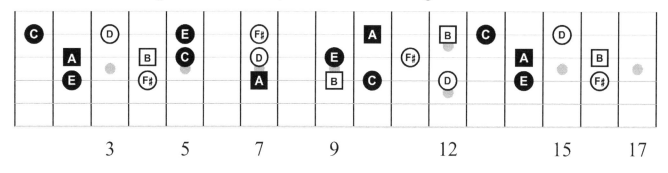

Am and Bm triad pairs on the 3rd, 2nd and 1st strings

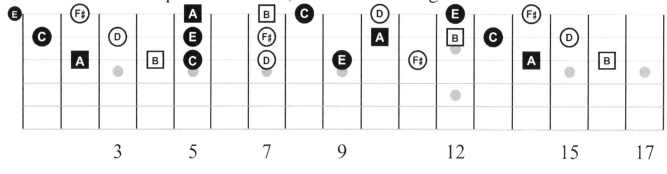

Over an A Minor chord, the Am (A C E) and Bm (B D F#) triad pair creates a *Dorian* tonality of 1 2 b3 4 5 due to the presence of the F# (the major 6th of Dorian). This triad pair doesn't contain the b7 of A Dorian, b does include the 9th (B).

Example 1h demonstrates an easy way to cut through octaves using shifting two-string minor triads. This for can easily be applied to major triad pairs too.

Example 1h:

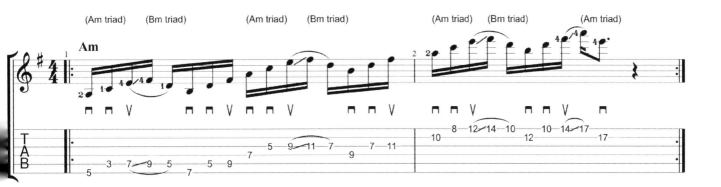

Using a more vertical layout, Example 1i creates a Dorian lick out of triad pairs between the 7th and 12th frets and avoids using the same shape twice in a row.

Example 1i:

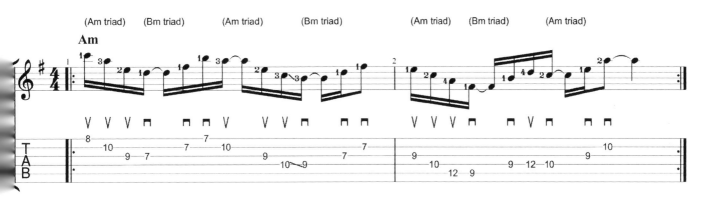

Over a B minor chord, the A Minor/B Minor triad pair evokes the Phrygian mode (1 b2 b3 4 5 b6 b7) with the C note in the A Minor triad supplying the minor 2nd degree of B Phrygian.

In B Phrygian,

The A Minor triad provides A (b7) C (b2/b9) and E (4/11)

The B Minor triad provides B (1) D (b3) and F# (5)

In Example 1j, the tension of the dissonant minor 2nd is released whenever the lick moves back into chord tones of the B Minor harmony. This is an acquired taste, so see what you think!

Example 1j:

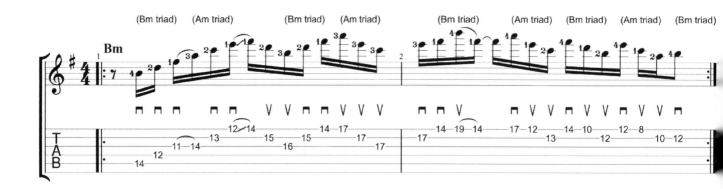

The A Minor/B Minor combo works well over a C major chord to outline Lydian and includes the tones 1, 2 3, #4, 6 and 7.

Over a D major chord, the A Minor/B Minor triads outline Mixolydian and include the tones 1, 2, 3, 5, 6, and b7.

Experiment with major and minor triad pairs over both C Major and D Major backings, and alternate betwee them in your improvisation.

Example 1k shows that even two-string melodies can create the triad pair sound. This lick is played over a C major chord to create a Lydian sound, but it works well over a D major chord too.

Example 1k:

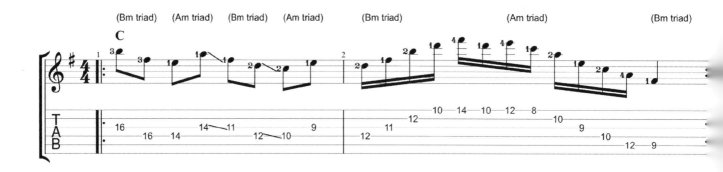

Example 1l, which is played over a D major chord, will sound great over either C major or D major chord Each unit of six notes uses three upstrokes and three swept upstrokes and downstrokes.

Example 1l:

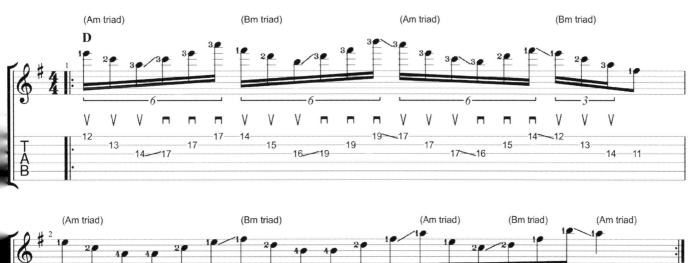

You don't often hear triad pairs over the VII chord in a major key, but the A Minor/B Minor pair over F#m7b5 creates a unique sound while avoiding the dissonance of the b2/b9 of F# Locrian (1 b2 b3 4 b5 b6 b7).

In context, the A Minor triad contains the b3, b5 and b7 intervals while the B Minor includes the 4/11, b6/b13 and 1 of the underlying chord.

Played in melodic groups of five in 1/16th note subdivisions, Example 1m has a displaced melodic feel, with triad changes moving further away from the downbeats until resetting in bar two, beat 2.

Example 1m:

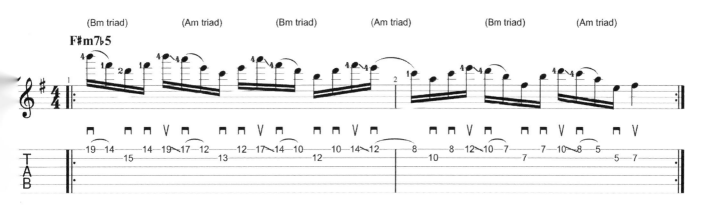

Mixed Triad Pairs

Pairing triads of different chord types allow us to express sounds that branch out from neighbouring major/ major and minor/minor examples to imply scales and modes beyond the major scale.

Still in the key of G Major, over an E minor (chord VI), a pairing of the VI (E Minor) and V (D Major) triads works well. The E Minor and D Major triads combine to give us the 1, 2, b3, 4, 5, b7 of E Aeolian. This happens to be the tonality created by the Cher song I mentioned in the introduction!

E Minor provides E(1) G(b3) and B(5)

D Major provides D(b7) F#(2/9) and A(4/11)

Example 1n features the E Minor/D Major triad pair in inversions stepping down the first three strings.

Example 1n:

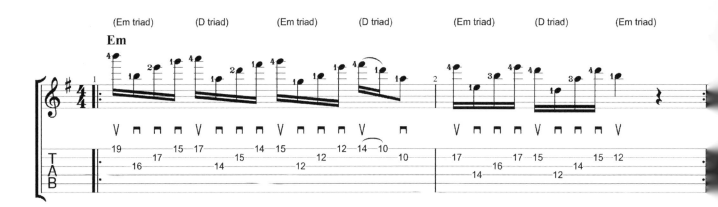

Example 1o takes an upward direction using a four-string approach and quintuplet note groupings.

Example 1o:

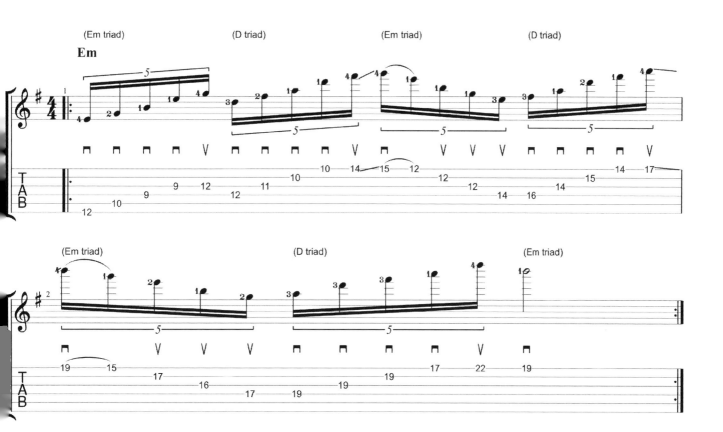

The previous two licks both sound interesting over an A minor chord too, since the E Minor/D Major triad pair contains the notes of A Dorian without the 3rd (C).

A mixed pair of A Minor and B Major (B, D#, F#) can be used to create the sound of E Harmonic Minor (1, 2, 3, 4, 5, b6, 7). Only the G (b3) is not included in the pair.

A Minor includes the notes A(4/11) C(b6/b13) E(1)

B Major includes the notes B(5) D#(7) and F#(2/9)

Example 1p is written in the style of Yngwie Malmsteen, using his picking approach to three-string triads. If you prefer *inside picking*, you can hit the G string in each triad with an upstroke and change direction heading back to the B string.

Example 1p:

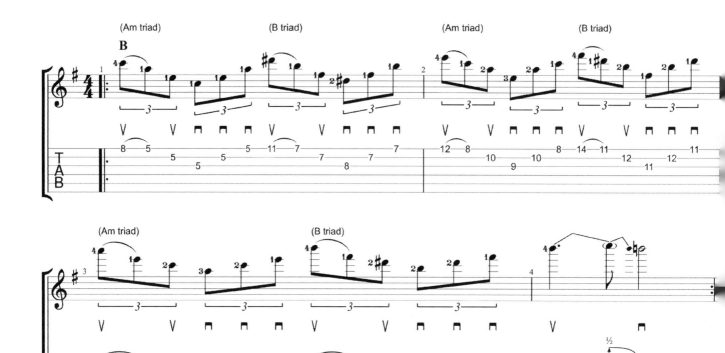

Over a B Major chord this pair outlines out the *Phrygian Dominant* mode *(*1 b2 3 4 5 b6 b7) perfectly. The A Minor triad creates tension and B the Major triad brings resolution.

A Minor contains A(b7) C(b9) and E(11/4)

B Major contains B(1) D#(3) and F#(5)

Using six-string shapes for both triads, Example 1q will test your ability to be smooth and accurate, so take your time with it and use inside picking and sweeps.

Example 1q:

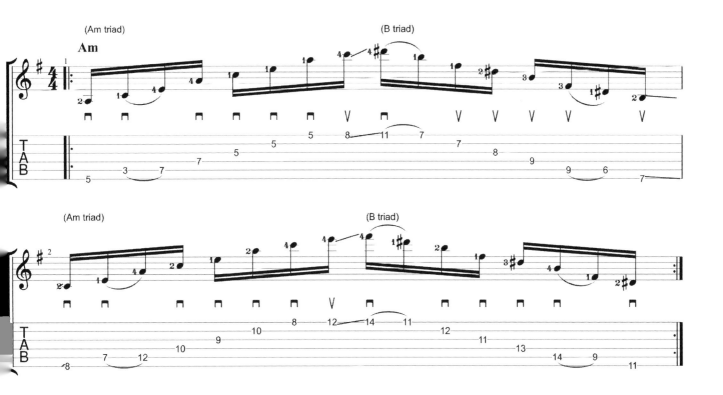

Another mixed triad pair for the E Harmonic Minor sound is made up of E Minor and D# Diminished (D#, F#, A) triads. Built on the major 7th degree of the harmonic minor, the D# Diminished triad functions like a B7 chord without the root note. Over an E minor chord, this creates an inside/outside sound as the diminished triad creates tension and the minor triad releases it.

Example 1r:

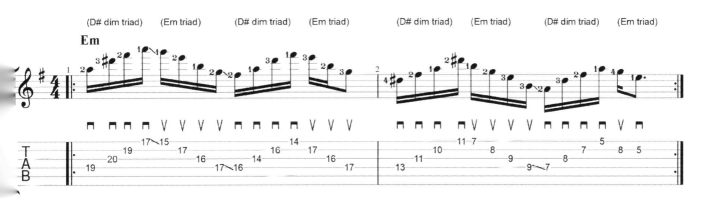

Example 1s, an unusual triad pair of F# Diminished (F# A C) and E Major (E G# B) triads is used over an F#m7b5 chord.

This time we're treating the F#m7b5 chord as the VI chord of A Melodic Minor (1, 2, b3, 4, 5, 6, 7), and using adjacent triads from that scale.

The G# in the E Major triad is a major 9th (instead of the more common minor 9th) of F#m7b5 and creates a Locrian Natural 9 scale. The two triads combine to create the sound of an F#m11b5 arpeggio.

Heard over an F#m7b5 chords, the two triads combine to give us the intervals,

F# Diminished F# (1) A(b3) C(b5)

E Major E(b7) G(9) B(4/11)

This sound is an acquired taste if you haven't played melodic minor before, but is very effective in creating a mysterious and unresolved tonality.

Example 1s:

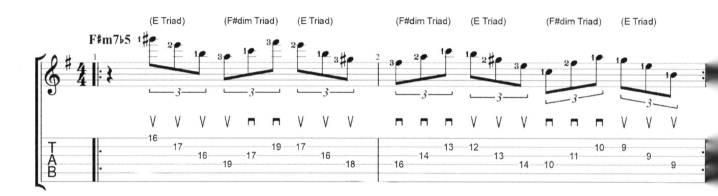

Any dominant chord (like D7) can also be treated as the IV chord of A Melodic Minor. By pairing a D Major triad (D F# A) with a C Augmented triad (C, E, G#), D Lydian Dominant (Lydian with a b7) is implied.

Over D7, the triads give us the intervals,

D Major Triad: D(1) F#(3) A(5)

C Augmented Triad C(b7) E(9) G#(#11)

Jazz players love to use this sound over unaltered dominant seventh chords because the augmented 4th (#11th) adds colour without rubbing against the 3rd of the chord.

Example 1t:

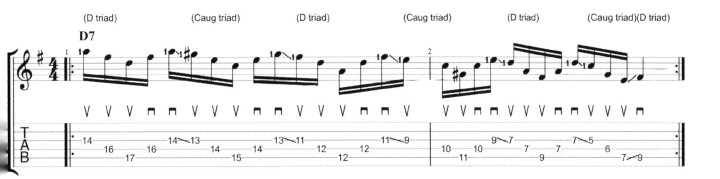

For a compelling altered chord sound, pairing up major triads a diminished 5th apart works a treat! While not a mixed triad pair *per se*, Example 1u combines D Major and Ab Major triads for a colourful, symmetrical sound that works perfectly over a D7 chord.

The tones of both triads (D, F#, A and Ab, C, Eb) belong to the *half-whole diminished* scale (D Eb F F# G# A B C) with G# being the *enharmonic equivalent* of Ab (same pitch, different name).

Combining these two triads implies a chord best described as D7b9(#11). Try this over the V chord in a IIm-V-I progression to build tension before a sweet resolution.

Example 1u:

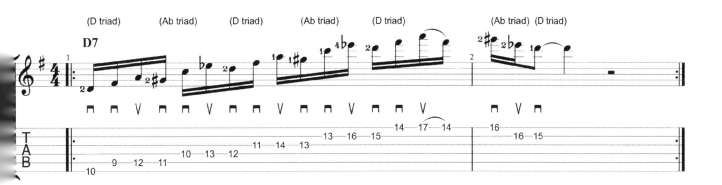

Chapter Homework: Triad Pairs

Practise each of the triad pairs in this chapter over the applicable backing tracks

Make a note of your favourite pairs over various chords

Compare your favourites to the summary table at the end of Chapter Two

See what other triad pairs you can come up with, either from the major scale or others

Write down the results, taking note of what you like or don't like about each

Focus on creating licks with your favourites, then applying them to improvisation

Triad Pair Etude

We close the chapter with a triad pair study piece. Passing through the chords E Minor, C Major, A Minor and B Major, the etude uses triad pairs that work over each chord. Emulate this approach with other chord progressions or jam tracks you improvise over.

Example 1v:

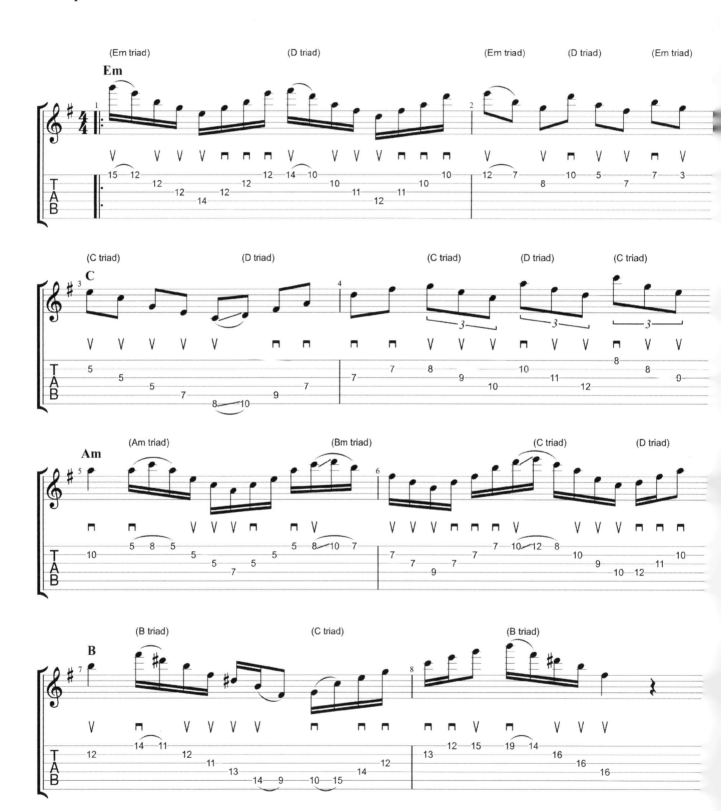

Chapter Two: Sassy Stacks and Substitutions

In this chapter, we'll be looking at another way to repurpose triads to create new sounds and how you can approach those options on the fretboard.

Triad Stacking

Triad stacking is a process where a base triad is used as a starting point for a series of other triads building in 3rds that can be used and combined over the original chord.

For example, beginning with a C Major triad from the key of G Major (C E G), we can repeatedly add diatonic 3rds to the top, and remove the note at the bottom to keep building new triads:

- C-E-G (C Major triad)
  - E-G-B (Removing the C and adding a B gives us an E Minor triad)
    - G-B-D (Removing the E and adding a D gives us a D Major triad)
      - B-D-F# (Removing the G and adding an F# gives us a B Minor triad)

Playing C Major and E Minor triads over a C chord implies a Cmaj7 arpeggio. Adding a G Major triad to the pair suggests Cmaj9, and adding a B Minor triad suggests Cmaj9#11 – a strong Lydian sound. The further you stack, the less stable the extension becomes as you move away from the original chord but, by connecting different triads in small pieces, a rich arpeggio sound can be imposed.

Example 2a:

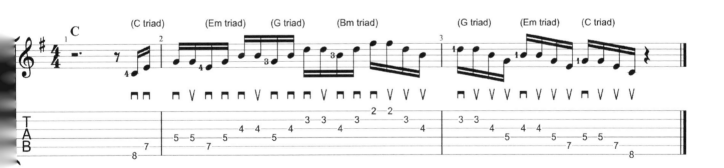

A word about *avoid* notes

Just as chord tones strengthen the connection between harmony and melody, some notes undermine that sturdiness by creating dissonance against chord tones. Such degrees are sometimes referred to by improvisers as *avoid* notes. However, rather than insisting you never play the avoid notes, I advise resolving them to chord tones and being careful with how much emphasis you give them. If you're just jamming over basslines, or ambiguous chords like root-5th power chords, then no notes are off limits.

When stacking and substituting triads over specific chord voicings, it's handy to be aware of avoid notes so that you can imply nice, musical extensions. Some chords withstand several extensions with triad stacks, whereas others will reveal clashes earlier on, stopping the process dead in its tracks if it exposes too much dissonance.

The following table lists stacks from each triad in the scale with ~~strikethroughs~~ used to denote the ones that contain avoid notes. The right-hand column describes the combined arpeggio sound created by each stack, excluding the eliminated triads. Later in the book, we'll look at some arpeggio shapes that avoid clashes by using omissions.

Root triad	3rd triad	5th triad	7th triad	Sounds like
G Major	B Minor	D Major	~~F# Diminished~~	Gmaj9
A Minor	C Major	E Minor	G Major	Am11
B Minor	D Major	~~F# Diminished*~~	~~A Minor*~~	Bm7
C Major	E Minor	G Major	B Minor	Cmaj9#11
D Major	F# Diminished	A Minor	~~C Major**~~	D9
E Minor	G Major	B Minor	D Major	Em11
F# Diminished	A Minor	~~C Major***~~	~~E Minor***~~	F#m7b5

* The minor 2nd (C) in these triads doesn't sit well as a melody note over a B Minor chord. Use it for a quick passing tone only.

** The G note in the C triad is an avoid note over a D chord. Using chords containing the F# (D, D7, D9) note you can stack triads up as far as the A Minor for a D9 sound. For voicings that omit the 3rd (D5 power chord, D7sus4, D11), stack the A Minor and C Major triads to imply a D11 arpeggio without any dissonance.

*** The minor 2nd G note in these triads sounds pretty ugly over diminished or half-diminished. The Locrian Natural 9 mode stacks a lot better.

The next seven examples show you some triad-stacking licks over 7th chords, based on the table above. I like to switch through triad stacks often to create a cascading effect, but you can experiment with bigger forms of any of the triads that you wish to superimpose over the accompanying chords.

Example 2b: Gmaj9 implied with triad stacks

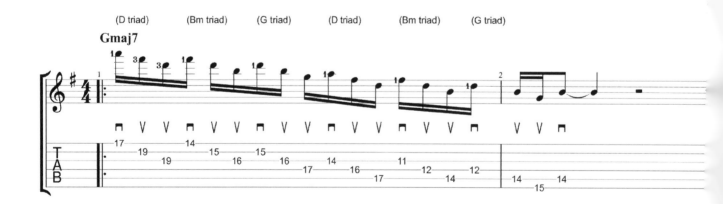

Example 2c: Am11 implied with triad stacks

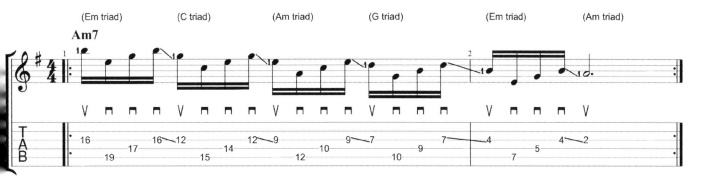

Example 2d: Bm7 implied with triad stacks

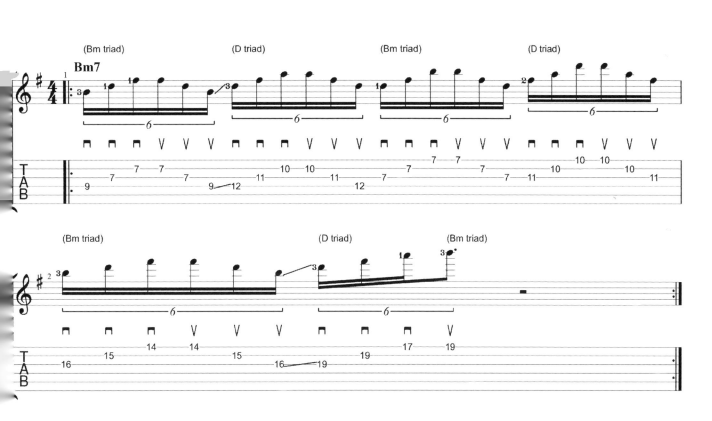

Example 2e: Cmaj9#11 implied with triad stacks

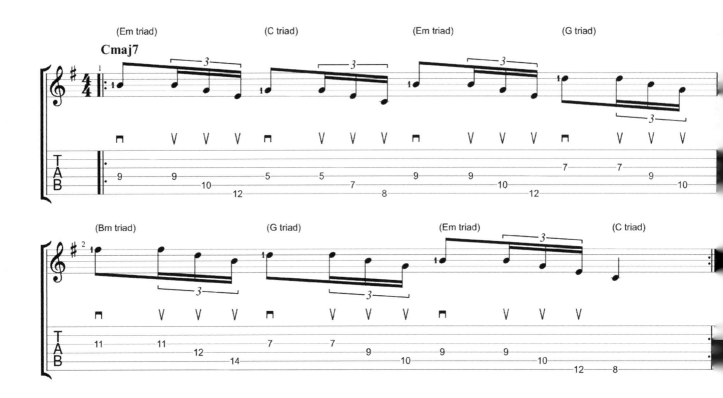

Example 2f implies a D9 arpeggio in bar one and a D11 in bar two. The C Major triad is used in bar two because the chord voicing (D7sus4) includes the note G.

Example 2f: D9 and D11 implied with triad stacks

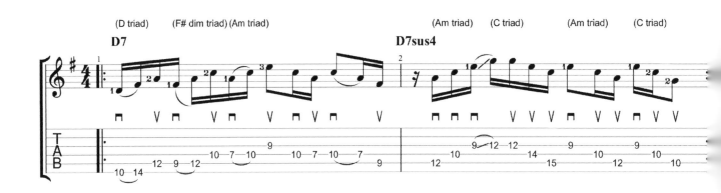

Example 2g: Em11 implied with triad stacks

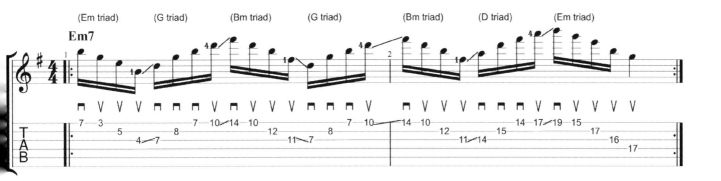

Example 2h: F#m7b5 implied with triad stacks

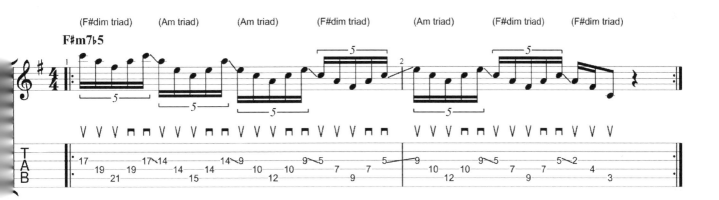

n other scales like the harmonic and melodic minor, diminished triads can extend in different ways to outline
im7 (1, b3, b5, bb7) or m11b5 (1, b3, b5, b7, 9, 11) arpeggios.

reating F#dim7 as a VII chord in G Harmonic Minor, Example 2i can be played over any diminished seventh
hord that begins on F#, A, C or Eb, including the D# of E Harmonic Minor. They are all inversions of each
ther because this chord contains minor 3rd intervals exclusively.

Example 2i: F#dim7 implied with triad stacks

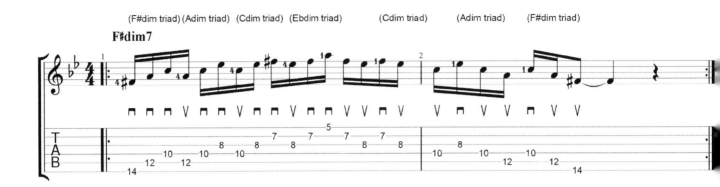

Using the Locrian Natural 9 mode, triad stacking is made possible up to three steps above the original triad outlining the F#m11b5 arpeggio referred to in Example 1s.

Example 2j: F#m11b5 implied with triad stacks

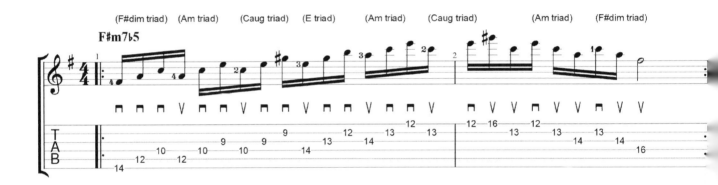

Vertical Triad Stacks

I often arrange triad stacks both above and below each other in string pairs to create positional sweep picking licks. I first heard Richie Kotzen use this kind of idea and decided to explore what other scale degrees it might work for.

Each vertical stack contains the root triad on the low E and A strings, the 7th triad on the D and G strings concluding with the 5th triad on the B and high E strings.

Example 2k is the original Kotzen pattern which creates an Am11 arpeggio sound over the accompanying chord. Each string pair is fretted with the second, first and fourth fingers. Move the lick up a perfect 5th produce the same effect for an Em11 arpeggio over chord VI (Example 2p).

Example 2k:

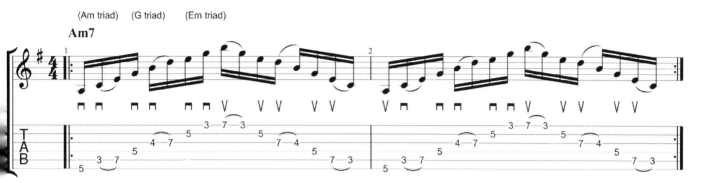

Going through the chord degrees of G Major in order, the I chord does not produce a successful vertical triad stack because of the dissonant F# Diminished triad over the G Major chord. Instead, I swap the C note for a B for a cool G Major ninth sound with the same picking mechanics as others in this series.

Example 2l: Customised vertical stack

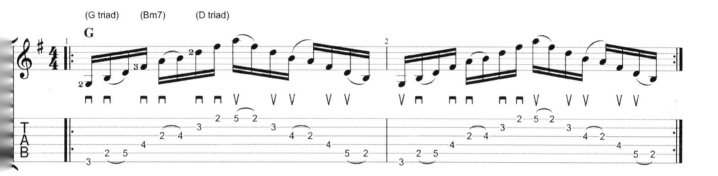

A vertical triad stack built around B Phrygian results in the avoid note being used twice in the triads B Minor, A Minor and F# Diminished. Instead, the mode's evil twin – B Phrygian Dominant (from the E Harmonic Minor scale) – creates a lovely dark sound when we stack B Major, A Diminished and F# Diminished triads to imply a B7b9 chord.

Why does this work even though there also are two C notes in this stack? As a functioning dominant chord, the B7b9's job is to build tension that will resolve in the I chord (E Minor in this case).

Example 2m:

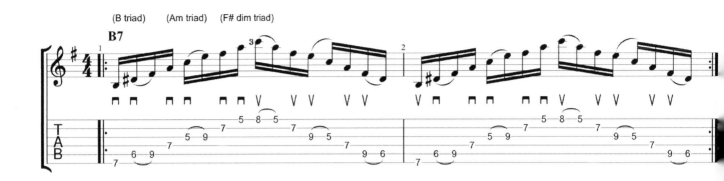

The IV chord stack is another one where I modify the layout, swapping the 1-2-1-2-1-2 notes per string formation for 2-1-2-1-2-1 to create a smoother fretting hand change from the lowest to middle triads.

Example 2n:

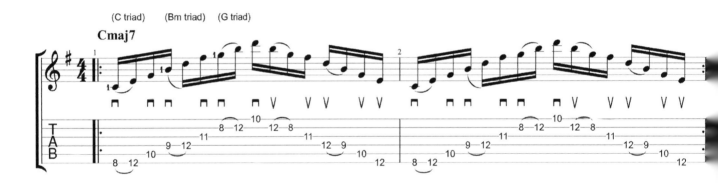

For the V chord and VI chord stacks, it's back to the 1-2 layout on each string pair. Example 2o includes the 11th of the chord (G) on the 12th fret of the G string in the first bar only. If this note sounds too suspended to your ears, replace it with the F# note one fret lower, as in bar two.

Example 2o:

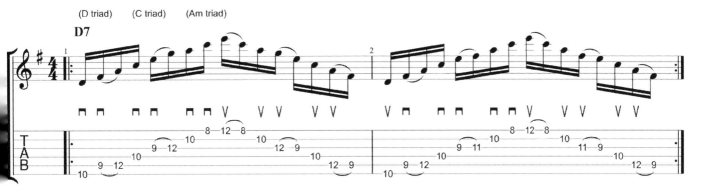

Example 2p is the same as Example 2k, but this time transposed a 5th higher to work over E minor chords.

Example 2p:

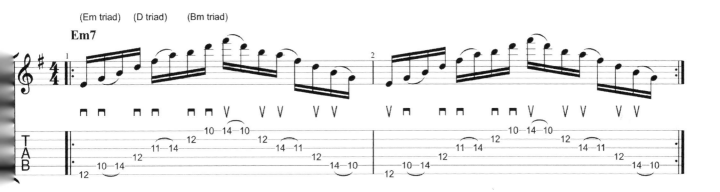

As an option on half-diminished chord vamps, I again suggest venturing into Locrian Natural 9 territory to stack F# Diminished, E Major and C Augmented triads. For all you *Sex and The City* fans, the first six notes of this shape (F#m11b5 when combined) are what composer Danny Elfman used at the end of the TV show's memorable opening theme.

Example 2q:

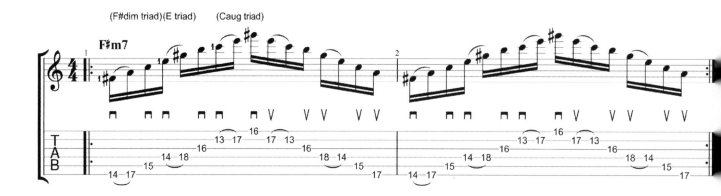

Seventh Arpeggio Stacking

The bigger an implied arpeggio becomes, the more ways there are to slice it up into bite-size pieces on the fretboard. For example, an Am11 arpeggio (A, C, E, G, B, D) could be implied with an A Minor/G Major triad pair, an A Minor/C Major /E Minior/G Major triad stack and – for the final device in this chapter – a seventh stack.

The Am11 example can be broken up into the seventh chords Am7 (A, C, E, G), Cmaj7 (C, E, G, B) and Em (E, G, B, D). I like to alternate the first and last of the three through two octaves.

Example 2r uses Am7 (black) and Em7 (grey) arpeggios, played in the ascending intervallic order of b7, 1, b3, 5, b7 and the opposite descending order. Shared notes are split-colour.

Am7 and Em7

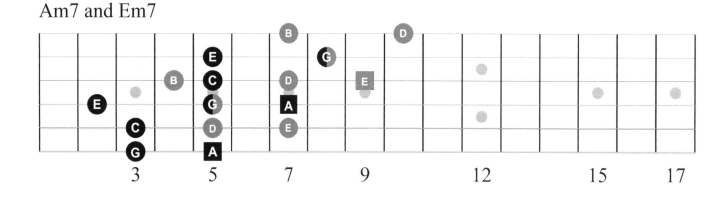

The overlap of E and G notes in both arpeggios make for a sequenced effect, as each ascending arpeggio the pair finishes on a higher note than the next begins. In the descent, each arpeggio concludes on a lower note than the starting one of the following arpeggio.

Example 2r:

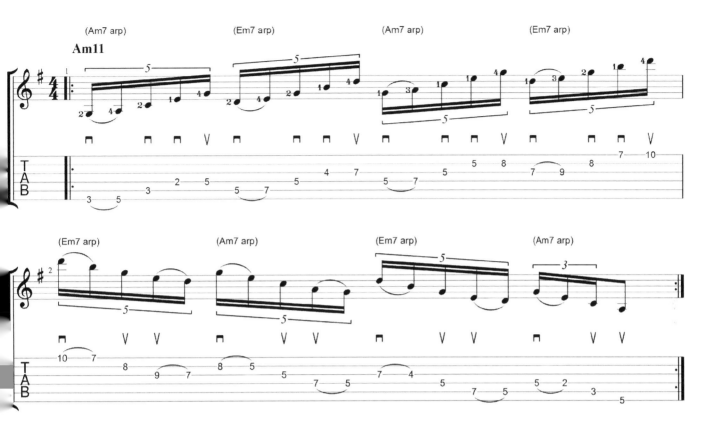

he same approach can be applied on the Em11 chord, using Em7 and Bm7 arpeggios to outline the larger
rpeggio. Try playing Example 2r a perfect 5th higher using the shapes below.

:m7 and Bm7

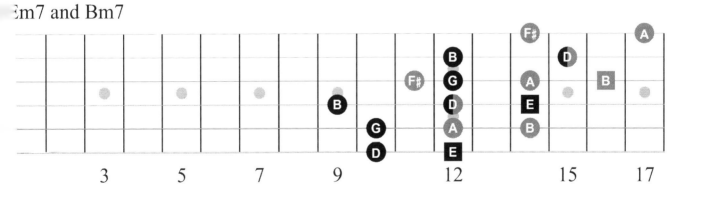

om chord IV of G Major, a Cmaj9#11 chord (C, E, G, B, D, F#) can be split into the shapes of Cmaj7, Em7
d Gmaj7 arpeggios. Using the Cmaj7 (black markers) and Gmaj7 (grey markers) results in a C Lydian lick
.e Example 2s.

Cmaj7 and Gmaj7

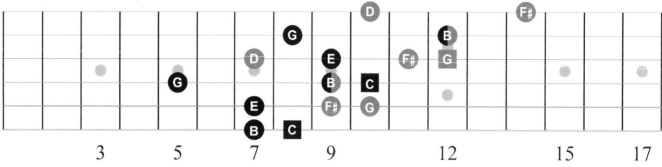

Example 2s:

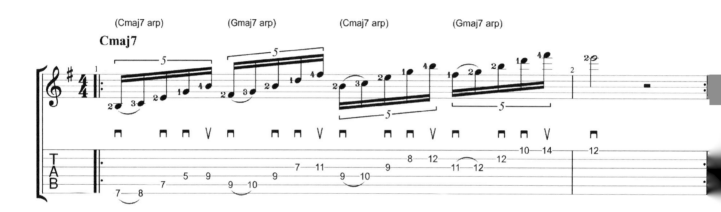

To evoke the upper extensions of dominant chords with seventh arpeggio stacks, try this approach over powe[r] chords, suspended dominants or voicings with no 3rd. In Example 2r, we used Am7 and Em7 arpeggios t[o] create an Am11 arpeggio. Used over a D bass note, the two seventh arpeggios outline a cool extended D13sus[4] chord. You can voice this chord by simply adding a B note to a D7sus4 chord:

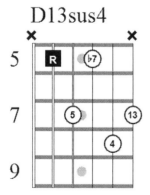

The notes of Am7 provide the 5, b7, 9 and 11, while the Em7 provides the 9, 11, 13 and root note of D13, to produce a sound that highlights the upper extensions.

Example 2t:

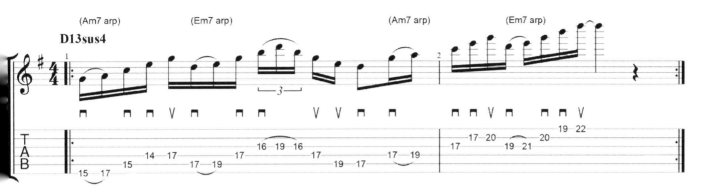

Poor old I chord hasn't had much love in this section, so here's a way to imply an extended chord like Gmaj13 by repeatedly stacking until you find the best option. Because the 11th (C) is an avoid note, my approach is to keep stacking seventh arpeggios until I move beyond the problem note.

G, B, D, F# = Gmaj7

B, D, F#, A = Bm7

D, F#, A, C = D7

F#, A, C, E = F#m7b5

A, C, E, G = Am7

C, E, G, B = Cmaj7

E, G, B, D = Em7

The Am7 and Cmaj7 arpeggios are ruled out because they contain C notes, but the Em7 arpeggio provides a way to access the highest extension (13th) by going beyond the avoid note.

Example 2u:

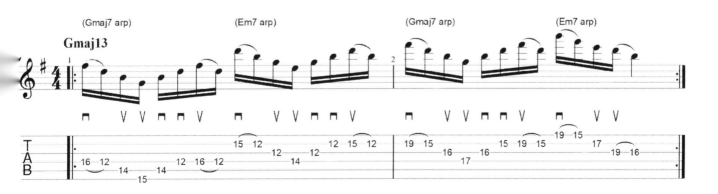

Arpeggios with upper extensions are tackled in more detail in Chapter Five, but for now, enjoy creating the sounds of extended chords by connecting the smaller arpeggio units contained in this chapter.

Summary of Pairs and Stacks

To summarise the melodic options for creating lines with arpeggios, here are my favourites as they apply to the key of G Major, and also some substitutions that have been discussed so far. When you've worked through all the material in this part of the book, assemble tables like this that include your favourite options.

Chris' Favourite Diatonic Options:

Base chord	Triad Pair	Triad Stack	Vertical Stack	7ths stack
G Major	-	G, Bm, D	G, Bm7*, D	Gmaj7, Em7
A Minor	C/D, Am/Bm	Am, C, Em, G	Am, G, Em	Am7, Em7
B Minor	Am/Bm	Bm, D	-	-
C Major	C/D, Am/Bm, Em/D	C, Em, G, Bm	C, Bm, G	Cmaj7, Gmaj7
D Major	D/C, Am/Bm	D, F#dim, Am	D, C, Am	Am7, Em7
E Minor	Em/D	Em, G, Bm, D	Em, D, Bm	Em7, Bm7
F# Diminished	Am/Bm	F#dim, Am	-	-

*a substitute chord fragment as explained in Example 21.

Favourite Substitutions:

Base chord	Triad Pair	Triad Stack	Vertical Stack	7ths stack
B7	B/Am, B/C	B, D#dim, F#dim, Adim, Cdim	B, Adim, F#dim	-
D7	D/Caug, D/Ab	D, F#dim, Am, Caug	D, Caug, Am	D7, Am(maj7)
F#m7b5	F#dim, E	F#dim, Am, E, Caug	F#dim, E, Caug	F#m7b5, Cmaj7#5

Chapter Homework: Stacks and Substitutions

- Pull up a one-chord backing track in the key of G Major from the audio download

- Try each of the options from the summary table

- By circling options in the book or writing them on a separate page, make a note of your favourite option

- Build your own licks using the choices you indicated above

- Repeat with the other chords

Chapter Three: Sequencing with Swagger

A melodic sequence is the repetition of a motif at a higher or lower pitch. In scale playing, sequences are a common way to break up a stream of consecutive scale notes while maintaining a general upward or downward direction.

Sequences are usually described in a way that reflects the content of each unit or step. For example, a 1-2-3-4 or *ascending fours* sequence in a G Major scale would see the notes ascending four notes from each note in the scale:

G A B C - A B C D - B C D E - C D E F# etc.

Sequencing Arpeggios

For arpeggios, sequencing is an effective method of breaking up chains of consecutive chord tones that are usually swept up and down in bursts. Since the one-note-per-string layout of many arpeggio shapes makes them potentially challenging to sequence, let's run through some useful strategies to determine which forms work best for which sequences.

Ascending and Descending Fours

One of my favourite arpeggio forms for ascending and descending fours is the Vertical Triad Stack concept used in Chapter Two. Many players will approach this sequence with alternate picking, but I like to take advantage of sweep picking and slurs where possible. These techniques give the sequence a smoother quality and sound less like a picking exercise.

Example 3a ascends in four-note steps using a triad stack of E Minor, D Major and B Minor triads. Bar one, beat 4 begins on a downstroke to mimic the picking of the previous three-beat cycle of the sequence.

Example 3a:

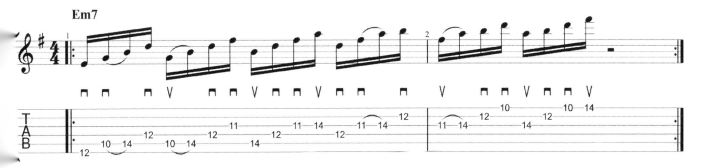

Even though the sequence works in units of four notes, it can be fun to phrase it in subdivisions of three. To try this, run through Example 3b which has the same notes and picking as the previous example but played as 8th note triplets.

Example 3b:

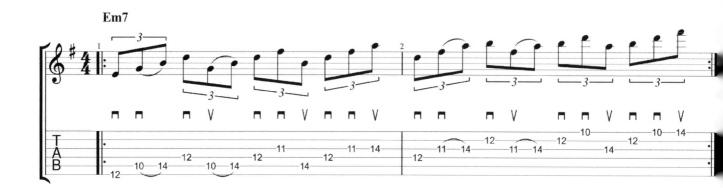

Using the same triad stack with descending fours, Example 3c is set up to take advantage of upward sweeping pick strokes, opposite to the way Example 3a was optimised for downstrokes.

Example 3c:

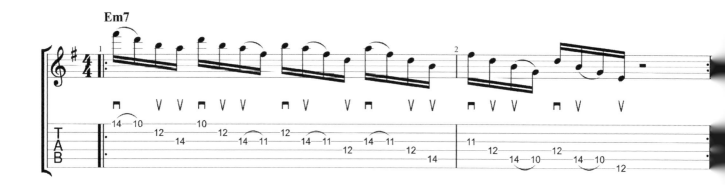

For regular major and minor triad shapes, ascending and descending fours can be troublesome. Take a look at Speed Shapes 1 and 2 for E Minor triads:

E Minor Speed Shapes 1 and 2

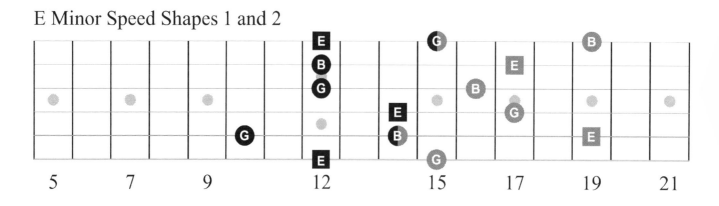

Individually, both shapes work well for sweep picking, but neither one is ideal for sequencing fours in either direction. Using Speed Shape 1 this way is fraught with finger rolling, and Speed Shape 2 finishes some steps on the same finger that the next would begin with.

As a practical alternative, I combine the two shapes into a position-shifting approach that's laid out in Example 3d. Bars one and two are designed for mostly downward sweeping through the ascending fours, with each group of four notes ending on an upstroke. Bars three and four descend through the same groups using a combination of upstrokes, downstrokes and pull-offs. Each of the pull-off notes could also be played with another upstroke.

Example 3d:

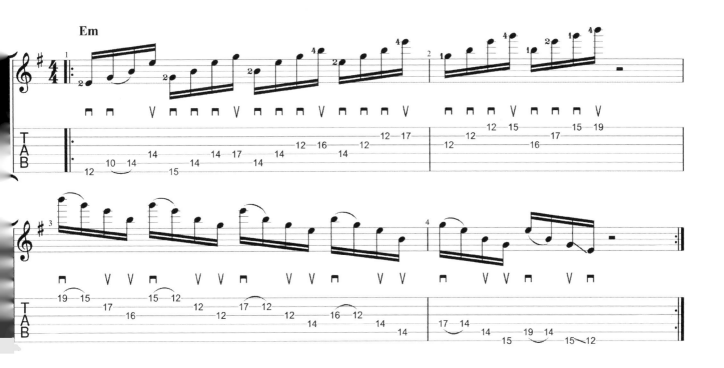

layers like Yngwie Malmsteen side-step the dilemma of sequencing large shapes by taking an exclusively horizontal approach to the arpeggio layout. Example 3e contains two bars of ascending fours and two bars of descending fours, covering almost the entire fretboard horizontally.

Example 3e:

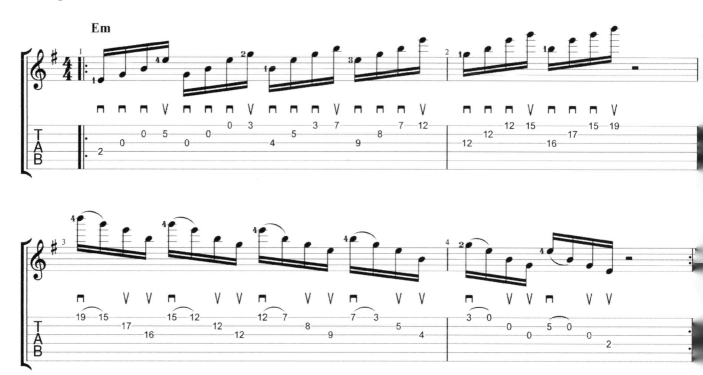

With a six-string C Major shape and some four-string inversions, Example 3f combines a regular sweep picking ascent and descent at either end with a middle section containing descending horizontal fours. It is reminiscent of neoclassical rock guitarists like Jason Becker.

Example 3f:

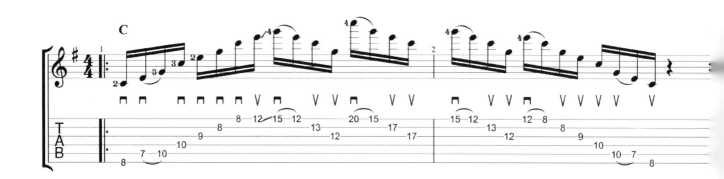

Ascending and Descending Threes

Three-note sequences work well with arpeggios because we only need to go back one step at the beginning of each new unit. You can alternate pick these examples but, once again, I've indicated an execution that takes advantage of any directional picking opportunities.

Example 3g uses a vertical triad stack centred around a C Lydian sound, using the same fingering for the notes as used in Example 2n. Bars one and two use ascending threes with a picking mechanic that repeats every three beats. Bars three and four descend in threes with a separate repeated picking mechanic that also repeats after three beats.

Example 3g:

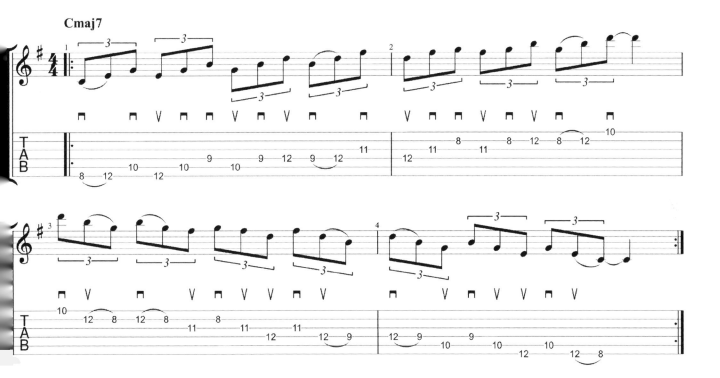

In garden-variety triads, the C-shape or Speed Shape 2 works well for sequences of threes. The effect is reminiscent of Vinnie Moore's early work, although Vinnie is equally likely to alternate-pick or *cross-pick* in his situation.

Example 3h:

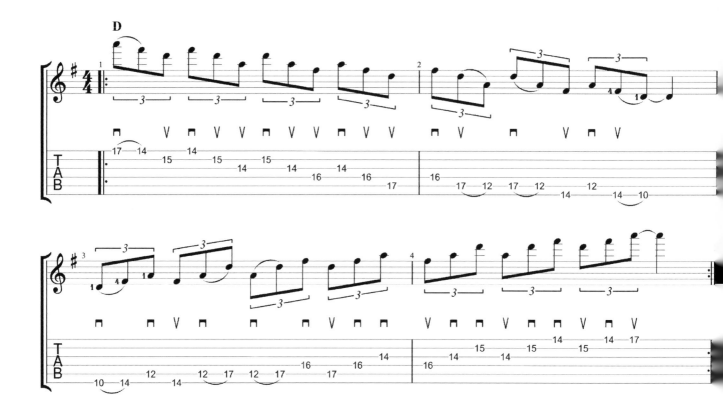

Different players often create their own ways to tackle the intricacies of picking technique. In the 1980s, Pa[u]l Gilbert found an excellent workaround for the annoyance of finger rolling in arpeggio playing by adopting *string-skipping* triad shapes. Pictured below, these shapes relocate the 5th degree from the B string to the [...] string.

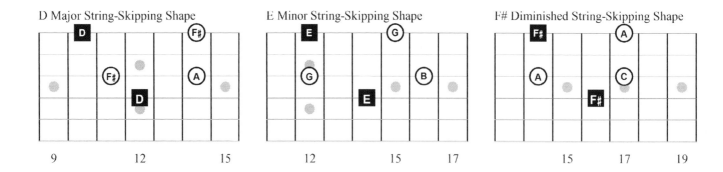

D Major String-Skipping Shape   E Minor String-Skipping Shape   F# Diminished String-Skipping Shape

With shapes like these, Gilbert found that he was more capable of sequencing speedy triad lines like descend[ing] threes. Example 3i uses a D Major triad, descending in three steps of three notes before a straight ascent ba[ck] to the start. Note that on the return to the beginning in bar two, the second iteration begins on an upstroke.

Example 3i:

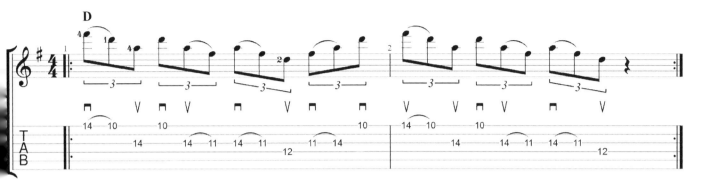

String-skipping shapes can be used in the midst of longer sequences too. In Example 3j, a couple of two-string units lead to some string-skipping on beats 3 and 4. From bar two, beat 2, more two-string units enable the sequence to continue further than the Gilbert shape.

Example 3j:

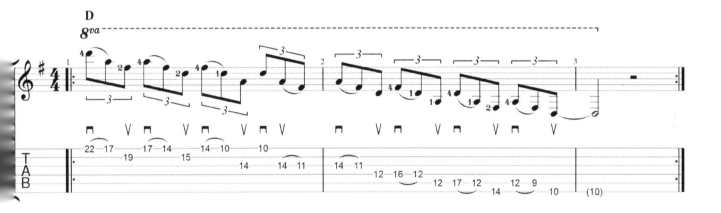

Another method I use to maximise the sequencing advantages of string skipping is to add an octave on a different set of strings. In Example 3k, the E Minor shape in 12th position can also be found starting on the B string in 5th position, an octave lower.

In the final 1/8th note triplet of bar two, beat 4, the E note has been repositioned to the G string, 9th fret in anticipation of what comes next. In bar three, beat 1, a small E Minor fragment on the D and G strings bridges the two string-skipping shapes to make it easier to get to the E note in beat 2 on the 14th fret with the second finger.

Example 3k:

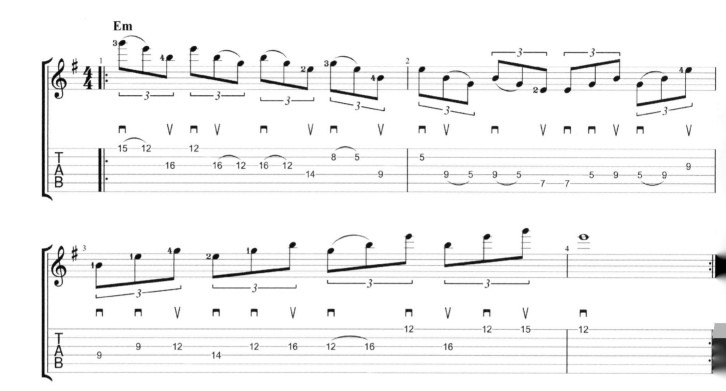

Alternating Twos

In scale terms, I usually refer to this sequence as a "thirds" sequence because it involves playing each sca[...]note and its diatonic 3rd in ascending or descending pairs. The ascending G Major scale played in 3rds wou[...]go G to B, A to C, B to D, C to E etc. In triad and arpeggio sequencing, we can similarly alternate the note[...]but the intervals won't be 3rds like they were in the scale. As such, let's call them "alternating twos".

Using a vertical stack of E Minor, D Major and B Minor triads with the notes E, G, B, D, F#, A, B, D, F[...]the ascending running order in Example 3l is E to B, G to D, B to F#, and so on. Bars three and four mov[...]downward through the alternating twos. As with all the sequences, you can go with my indicated pick strok[...]or good old alternate picking.

Example 3l:

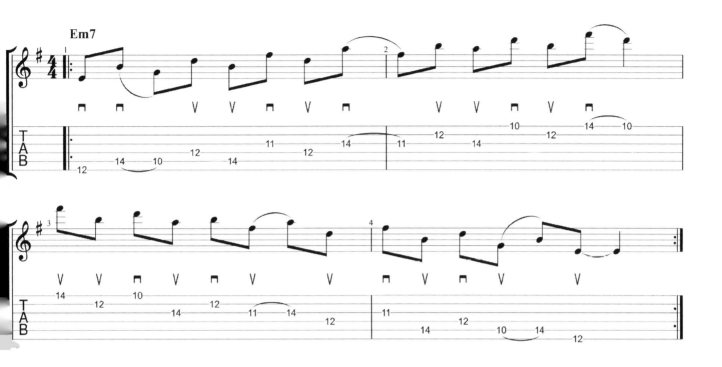

Often, string changing with alternate picking and a mostly one-note-per-string layout can be a challenge. There's nothing wrong with a challenge, but this wouldn't be a Chris Brooks book if I didn't offer you some handy alternative! Check out Example 3n for my spin.

Example 3m:

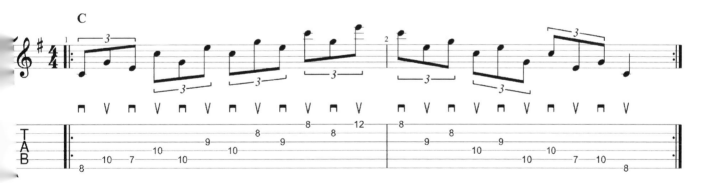

this version, each four-note unit occurs in a different position, taking the idea right up to the 20th fret of e high E string. In both directions, the picking is set up to take advantage of several two-string sweeps with picking mechanic of *down, down, hammer-on, up*. Pay close attention to where the position shifts occur in rs three and four, as there is some quick index finger work required.

Example 3n:

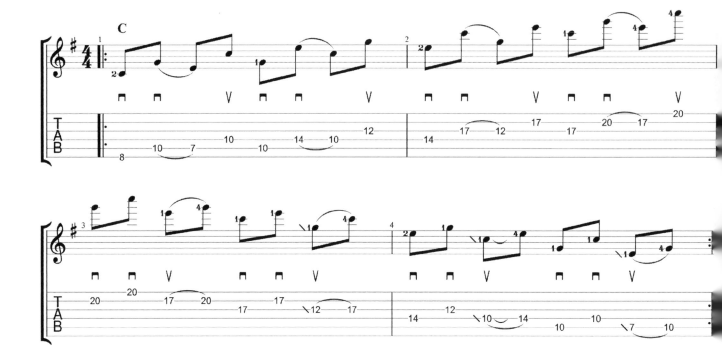

Five and Two Sequences

To imitate a harp-sounding cascade, try this seven-note sequence comprising five notes down and two back up. Each unit begins one chord degree lower than the previous step, and the sequence is used three times before the ending part of the lick that starts in bar two, beat 1 on the last 1/16th note.

Example 3o:

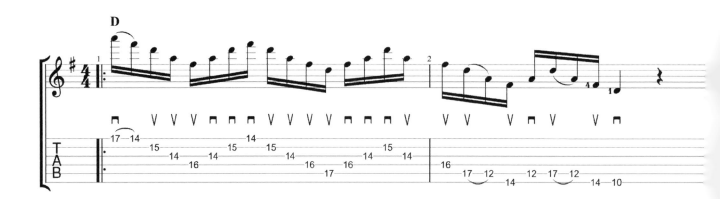

Example 3p works the opposite way to the previous example with five ascending notes and two descending notes in each unit of the sequence.

Example 3p:

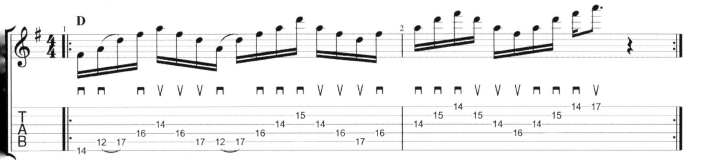

Tapping Threes

By using the fretting hand to outline one inversion of a chord and the other hand to finger tap extensions, an exciting approach to descending and ascending threes is born. Prevalent on the early albums of Greg Howe, this post-Van Halen approach to tapping works by beginning each unit of three notes with a tap, then two notes from the fretting hand.

All fretting hand notes are executed by pull-offs, hammer-ons and *hammers from nowhere*. A hammer from nowhere is simply a hammer-on used for the first new note on a string, rather than a slur from a previous lower note.

Before working on Example 3q, use this diagram to locate and tap out the grey notes with your picking hand. You'll only need one tapping finger like the index or middle finger.

C Major Tapping Sequence

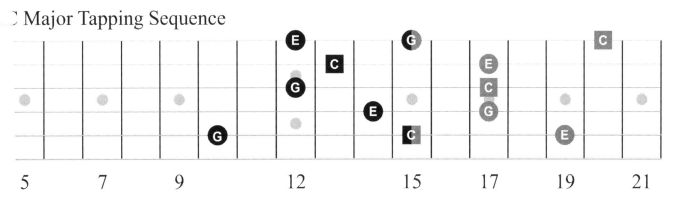

Example 3q:

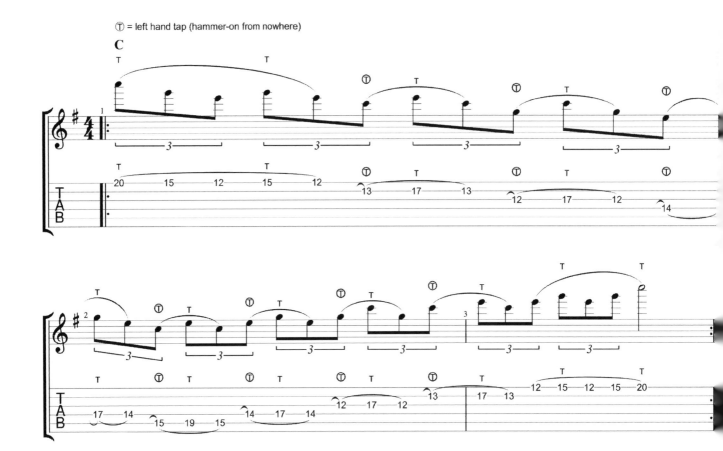

Here's my own little twist on the Greg Howe approach: tapping the notes of a different triad altogether t[o] create a fast hybrid arpeggio sound. For Example 3r you will use the same triad shape in both hands, but th[e] higher register will outline a G Major triad amongst the fretted C Major triad notes.

Example 3r:

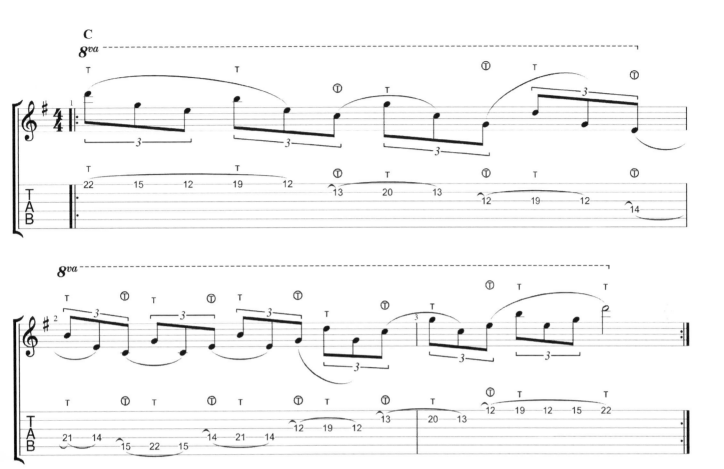

Displacement and Permutation

Rhythmic displacement is a powerful tool to get maximum mileage out of sequences and multiply the sounds available from a given sequence. A melody is displaced when it is moved to a different portion of a beat or bar. I use the terms *forward displacement* to describe phrases brought forward in time, and *backward displacement* for phrases pushed back until later.

In Example 3a, each unit began on a beat of the bar. By displacing where each step of a sequence starts, the ear will perceive a different sequence. What's more, you can create this effect without changing the picking mechanics in each displacement.

Example 3s contains the same notes as Example 3a, but begins one 1/16th note before the main bar (bar two). The note pushed across to the previous bar now acts as a pickup note for a new 1-2-3-1 sequence.

Example 3s:

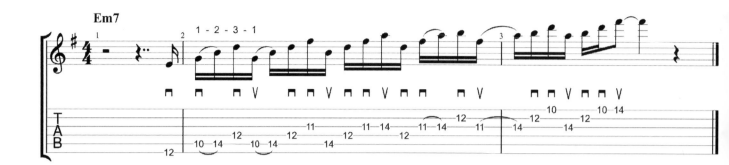

Displacing the note set by one more 1/16th to the left and then taking stock of the first four notes in bar two, we can see a 2-3-1-2 sequence.

Example 3t:

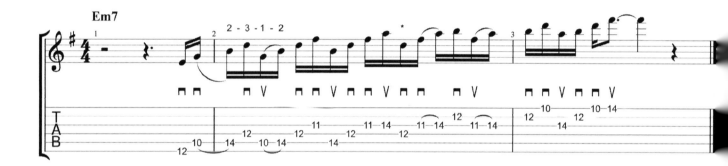

Repeating the process one more time with three pickup notes, Example 3u is a 3-1-2-3 sequence. Moving one more note to the left of the second bar would revert the sequence back to straight ascending fours.

Example 3u:

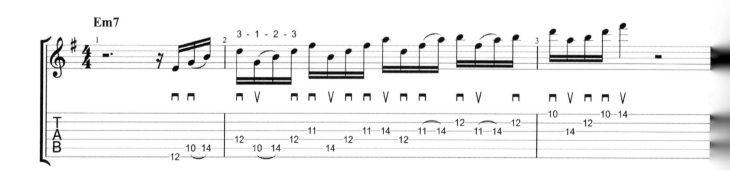

Backward displacement can be implemented by pushing phrases to the right within the bar using either spaces or extra notes. Based on the notes of Example 3n, the next example displaces an alternating twos sequence by adding an 1/8th note to the beginning of bar one. Playing an upstroke for the extra note means the picking from Example 3n can remain the same.

Example 3v:

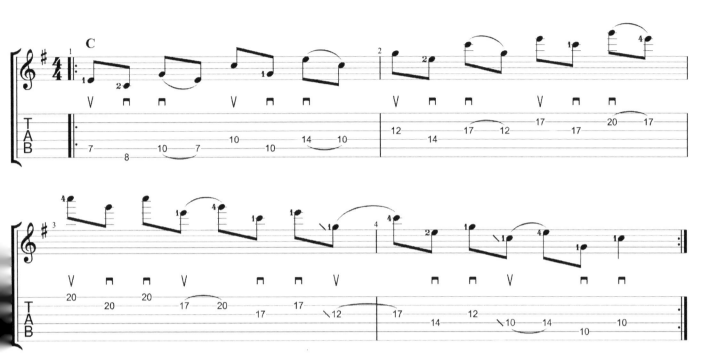

With a backward displacement of two 1/8th note triplets, the descending threes E Minor string-skipping sequence in Example 3w might challenge your timing. Be sure to work on it slower than your best non-displaced tempo and increase the speed only when you have a strong rhythmic grasp of where the notes now fall.

Example 3w

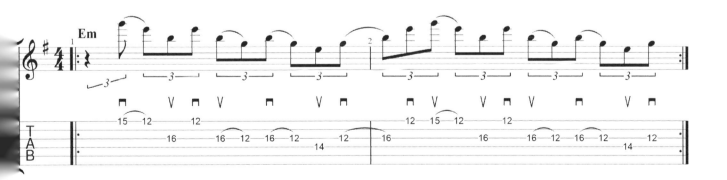

Composing is often an effective way work on things that might not come naturally in improvisation, so make a point of writing sequenced licks that move through chord progressions like this one in G Major.

Example 3x:

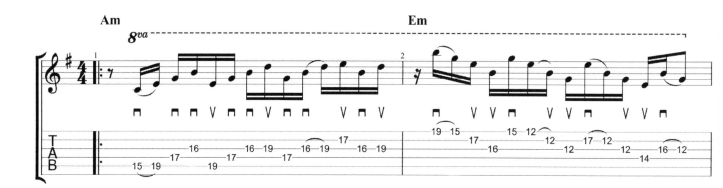

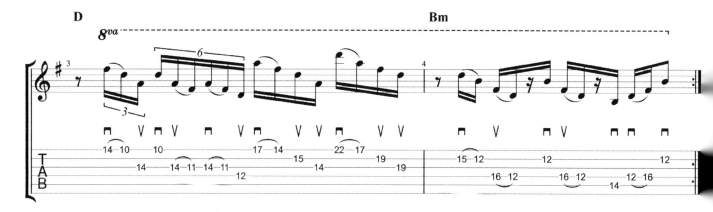

Chapter Homework: Sequences and Permutations

Bullet-pointing everything you've studied in this chapter reveals quite a lot of homework.

- *Ascending fours*

- *Descending fours*

- *Ascending threes*

- *Descending threes*

- *Alternating twos*

- *Five and two cascades*

- *Forward displacements*

- *Backward displacements*

To create practice sessions based on this material, I suggest limiting yourself to one or two related subjects per sitting using one arpeggio shape per session. Choose a couple of associated exercises that challenge you, then build a practice plan out of them.

Basing a practice session on Examples 3a and 3c might look something like this:

- Play the E Minor triad stack in ascending fours in free time – eight repeats

- Try it with a metronome at different speeds, aiming for six clean repeats at each tempo

- Repeat step 2 for each of the forward displacements – one, two and three pickup notes

- Repeat steps 1-3 for the descending version (Example 3c)

On the next day, you could follow a similar route to conquer the positional and horizontal approaches in Examples 3d, 3e and 3f, for instance.

When you have established a good command of four-note sequences, move on to ascending and descending threes, alternating twos etc. Start by batching together the relevant exercises in the book, but create your own licks as soon as you're able to.

Don't worry if not all sequences result in high-speed arpeggio licks, since some ideas can have even the best of us knotted up! Exploration through practice will give you a sense of which approaches work best for each arpeggio form. Encountering roadblocks can also inspire you to innovate your way out of tight spots, so persevere with the ideas that musically interest you, and the technique will catch up.

Most importantly, remember that a good practice session is a purposeful session. Just like a visit to the gym is wasted by walking around aimlessly to different machines, a practice session without a plan is a poor use of your time.

Write down what you hope to achieve each day, then go for it!

Chapter Four: Merge Scales Like A Boss

One of the most creatively-challenging aspects of arpeggio playing is fusing it purposefully with the other elements of your style. There's a genuine risk of arpeggios sounding disjointed from your other ideas. You've probably heard (or even been guilty of) a sweep picking idea that seemed out of place with what came before or after it. Don't worry. It's part of the process.

Two common causes of that disconnected sound are:

- Not knowing scales and arpeggios in the same area of the fretboard

- Focusing on developing both independently without regard for how to connect them

This chapter will take you through a three-step process I've found useful to integrate arpeggios and scales. By treating triads as a framework for scale notes, you'll see how they relate to each other and begin to build a vocabulary of connected ideas.

1. *Associate* an arpeggio with a nearby scale pattern

2. *Alternate* between an ascending arpeggio, a descending scale and the reverse

3. *Decorate* with sequences and variations

Scale Picking Approaches

It will be useful to understand the three picking approaches I employ for scale and lick playing to connect with sweep picking portions of arpeggios.

1. *Alternate Picking:* This picking approach uses opposing pick strokes – *down, up, down up* – based on where notes fall in a beat rather than how the line is laid out on the guitar. When rests or longer notes occur, the pick strokes resume their beat-based application as though the phrase were uninterrupted.

1. *Economy Picking:* Like sweep picking, economy picking affects the way string changes are handled. Whenever the pick can leave one string and arrive at the next string with the same directional pick stroke, it is done with a sweep, mostly where licks have odd numbers of notes per string.

2. *Compound Picking (The Yng Way)*: Based on the approach in my book *Neoclassical Speed Strategies for Guitar*, the final picking style is optimised for a *downward picking orientation* (DPO), making the most of ideas that begin strings on downstrokes. This system uses economy picking for ascending string changes, alternate picking for even-numbered lines, and a combination of alternate picking and slurs for descending lines.

Even though the scalar examples are notated with pick strokes that *I* find useful for each of the phrases ahead, my advice is to use the one that is most comfortable and expressive. If you're in the market for a speed picking system, however, I recommend *Neoclassical Speed Strategies*!

Alternate Picking

Economy Picking

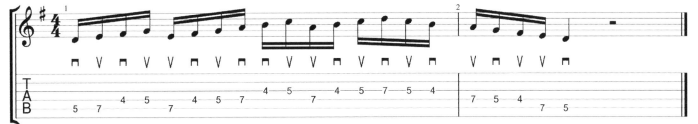

Compound Picking

tep One: Associate

llustrating an example of chord tones within a scale pattern, Figure 4a highlights the notes of a G Major riad (black markers) inside a G Major scale. This is how I suggest you try to visualise chord tones and their urrounding scale notes.

igure 4a:

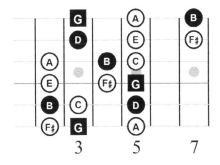

Scale and arpeggio diagrams often overlap perfectly as they did in Figure 4a. In other cases, they may deviate to improve fingering convenience.

Since there are seven notes in a major scale, a widespread method of fretboard coverage uses seven *three-note-per-string* (*3nps*) patterns. In G Major, the lowest moveable pattern starts on the 7th of the scale (F#).

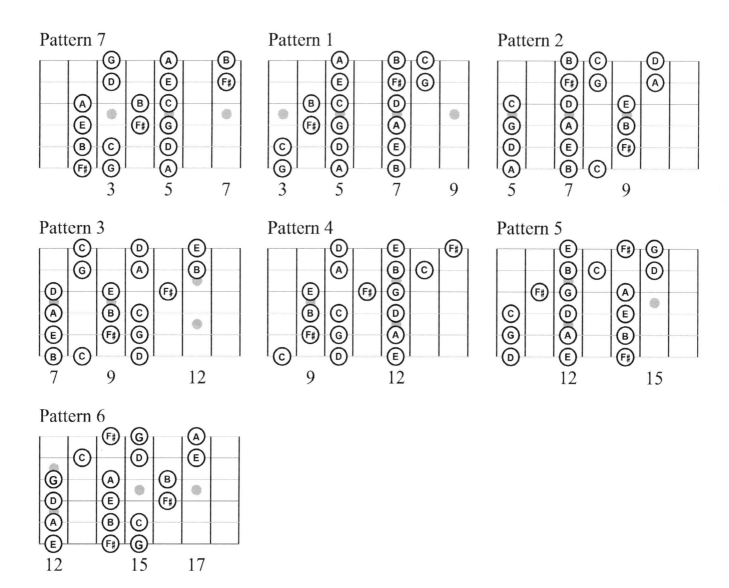

You can use any scale layout you like for these concepts, but the 3nps patterns are an excellent fit for tria shapes like the Speed Shapes covered in *Sweep Picking Speed Strategies* and referenced throughout thi chapter.

Using three sweep picking patterns per chord type (root position and two inversions), here are examples c major, minor and diminished triads from the key of G Major, matched with the closest 3nps scale pattern.

Figure 4b: G Major triads matched with scale patterns:

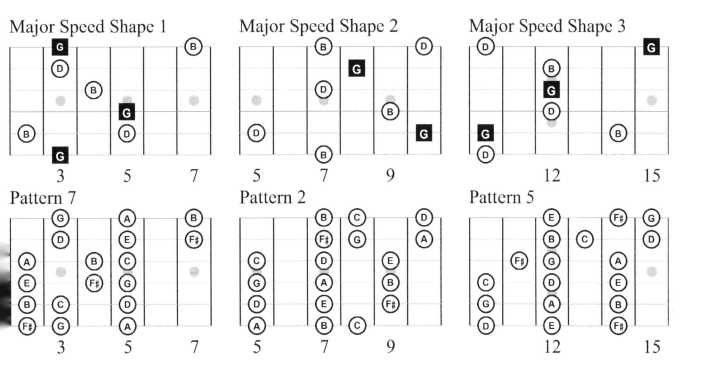

Major Speed Shape 1

Major Speed Shape 2

Major Speed Shape 3

Pattern 7

Pattern 2

Pattern 5

Figure 4c: A Minor triads matched with scale patterns:

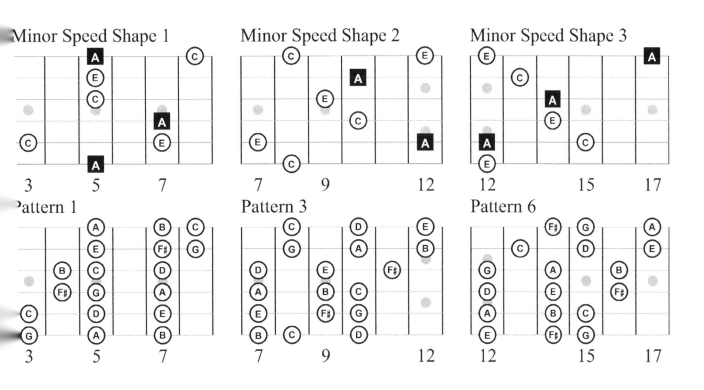

Minor Speed Shape 1

Minor Speed Shape 2

Minor Speed Shape 3

Pattern 1

Pattern 3

Pattern 6

When altering minor triads to create diminished triads, the misalignment of the flat 5th degree produces some shapes that, depending on the key and fretboard position, border on impractical. Many players will use fragments of these shapes rather than six-string sweep patterns.

Since many improvisers extend beyond the triad to use half-diminished and diminished seventh arpeggios instead, here are some suitable shapes for half-diminished or minor seventh flat five shapes. The 7th degree not only enriches the tonality, but bridges any awkward fretting between the flat 5th degree and the next root note up. Scale shapes 7 and 4 have been modified to integrate with the new arpeggio shapes.

Figure 4d: F# Half-diminished triads matched with scale patterns:

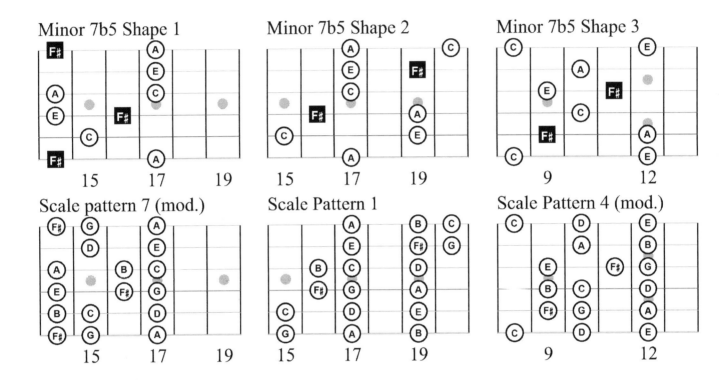

Triad / Scale Matrix

Since major scale harmony contains three separate major and minor triads each, it's important to know how scale patterns change from chord to chord and inversion to inversion. The in-between notes are what make minor tonality Dorian, Phrygian or Aeolian and a major tonality Ionian, Lydian or Mixolydian.

To expand on Figures 4c, 4d and 4e, the table below outlines suggested scale patterns for each triad shape i the key.

In Step Two, you can use this list to apply each example to every triad and inversion.

Chord Degree	Triad Shape 1	Triad Shape 2	Triad Shape 3
I (G Major)	Scale Pattern 7	Scale Pattern 2	Scale Pattern 5
II (A Minor)	Scale Pattern 1	Scale Pattern 3	Scale Pattern 6
III (B Minor)	Scale Pattern 2	Scale Pattern 4	Scale Pattern 7
IV (C Major)	Scale Pattern 3	Scale Pattern 5	Scale Pattern 1
V (D Major)	Scale Pattern 4	Scale Pattern 6	Scale Pattern 2
VI (E Minor)	Scale Pattern 5	Scale Pattern 7	Scale Pattern 3
VII (F#m7b5)	Scale Pattern 7	Scale Pattern 1	Scale Pattern 4

Step Two: Alternate

Time for some practical work! Let's cherry-pick examples from the Triad / Scale Matrix and work them through some combination drills. When you have them down, refer back to the matrix to substitute other matching scale and triad patterns.

Example 4a uses sweep picking to ascend through a G Major triad (Speed Shape 2) and compound picking to descend through the second scale pattern of G Major. Playing it as written means both bars can be handled with a downward pick slant without any reason to change picking orientation.

Example 4a:

Using the same triad shape for a C chord, note how the scale pattern differs in Example 4b.

Example 4b:

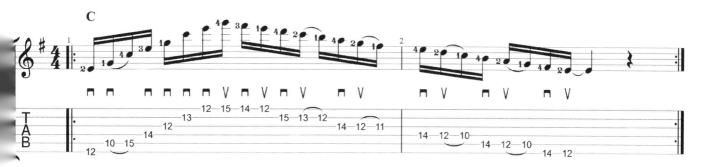

63

Reversing the order of the previous drills with a descending triad and an ascending scale, Example 4c uses the first speed shape of a G Major triad and the seventh scale pattern. Try this order with Examples 4a and 4b too.

For picking, I use an upward pick slant for the sweep portion, and downward-slanted economy picking for the scale.

Example 4c:

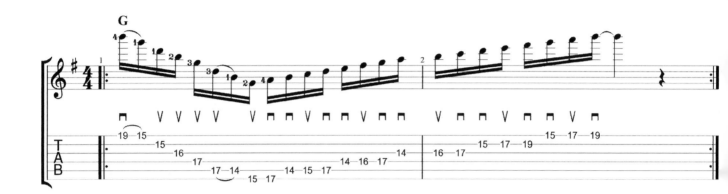

Using inversions enables *voice leading* through chord changes with triads. The second speed shape of D Major with the sixth scale pattern creates a very musical way of linking up Examples 4c and 4d. Try them individually and then combined.

Example 4d:

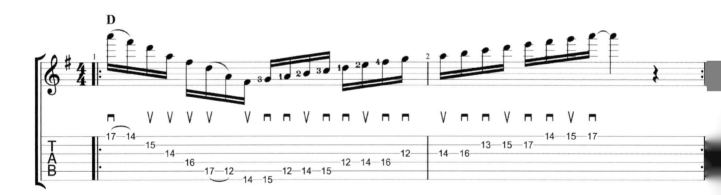

Before moving forward, try other combinations from the Triad / Scale Matrix, then proceed to the next few examples that use more than one chord in each drill.

Combining a six-string B Minor triad, a four-string A Minor triad and a five-string E Minor triad, Example 4 demonstrates the kind of seamless position shifting possible when linking triads and scales.

Example 4e:

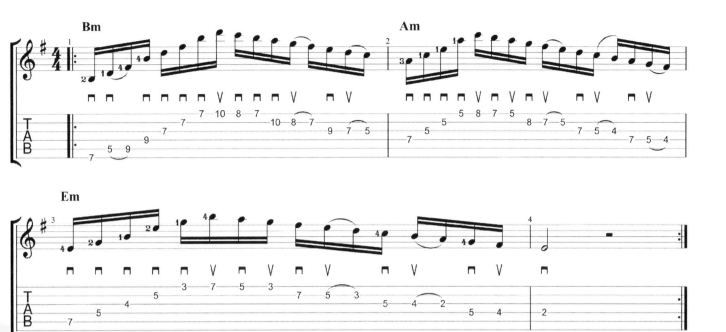

Let's try one more chord progression example before moving to Step Three. In Example 4f, scale portions are again used to create smooth transitions between triads in the progression. You can use as much or as little of a scale pattern as you find necessary to link up chord tones. This example uses a mix of three-, two- and five-string scales to get to each new chord in time for the next bar.

Example 4f:

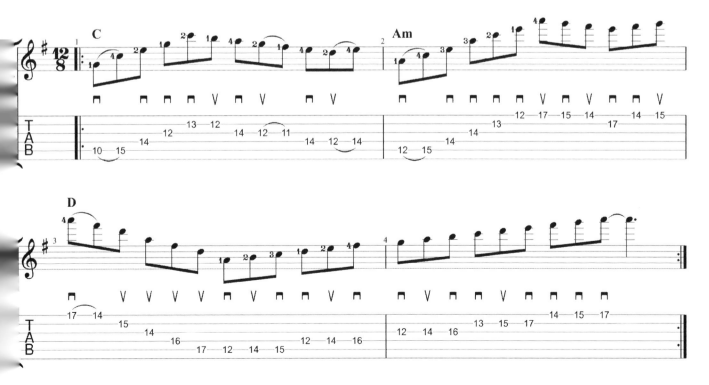

Step Three: Decorate

Rather than using triads and scales straight up and down, these examples use sequences and alternating directions to provide more interest. This is where real licks that transcend exercises come into play.

Example 4g weaves in and out of the second G Major triad shape and the second 3nps scale pattern. A simple way of breaking up consecutive scale notes is to double back to a previous string, which occurs in this example on beat 3 of each bar.

Example 4g:

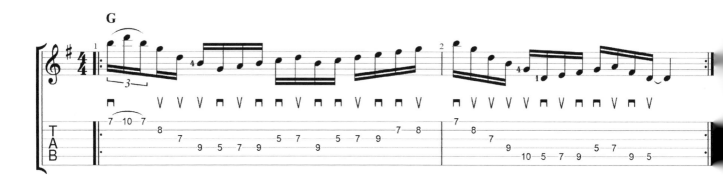

In Example 4h, a six-string A Minor triad in Speed Shape 2 is broken up into pieces using scale fragments played in descending 3rds in bar one, and with ascending passing notes in bar two. Even just a couple of notes like the D note (5th fret of the A string) between chord tones can break up the triadic sound.

There are many ways in which to tackle the picking of this lick, so experiment with the three picking types and the mixtures of approaches that I've designated.

Example 4h:

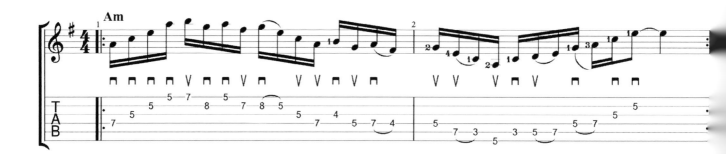

One of my favourite sequences for 3nps scales is what I call 2-3-1, in which three notes on a string are played in the order of middle, highest and lowest pitch. It works great for all kinds of picking and legato. In Example 4i, the 2-3-1 idea is used to break up a six-string C Major triad in three portions that occur from bar one, beats and 4, and bar two, beat 3. This has a textbook Lydian sound but try transposing it to other modes once you've memorised the form of the lick.

Example 4i:

Example 4j begins bar one with scale notes for a change, initiating an F#m7b5 arpeggio at beat 3. Bar two is framed within the arpeggio and, despite the scale sound of the legato passage in beat 1, only the B note on the high E string and the G note on the D string are outside of the chord tones.

Since the F#, A and C notes of an F# diminished triad also work as the 3rd, 5th and 7th of a D7 chord, try this example as a Mixolydian line over a V chord for another chance to apply it.

Example 4j:

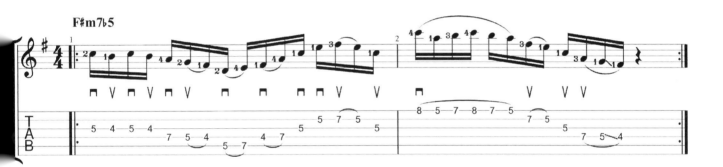

You can find more scale and arpeggio licks at the end of Chapter Five.

Chapter Homework: Triad and Scale Integration

Revise the *Speed Shapes* in each chord type presented

Learn the seven 3nps shapes of the G Major scale

Study the *Triad / Scale Matrix* and practise Step Two (*Alternate*) for each degree of the scale. Since there are seven modes, you might like to try memorising one row of the table per day

Ascend using each triad shape and descend using a nearby scale pattern

Descend using each triad and ascend using an adjacent scale pattern

- Transpose all the licks in this chapter to other modes within the key. Transcribing them on paper or in a transcription program will make it easier for you to keep them on hand for your practice.

- Try to create your own licks comprised of triads and scales

Chapter Five: Snazzier and Jazzier

In Part One of the book, we used small units of triads and seventh arpeggios as substitutes to create 9ths, 11th and 13th chord extensions. In this chapter, we're going to explore those arpeggios as full shapes in their own right and explore where they can be used.

You can utilise the ideas in this chapter when you come across exotic chords, such as a Cmaj13#11 or similar, but also when playing over simpler chords in order to add those upper extension "expensive" notes.

When arpeggiating chord types that have higher extensions beyond the first octave, these extensions occur in the second octave of the arpeggio and are literally laid out 1 3 5 7 9 11 13 on the fretboard.

In this chapter, the diagrams show the intervals rather than specific note names, and all the arpeggios start from the same root note. Each chord diagram is labelled with the degree(s) of the scale it applies to. Let's begin with major chords, using the format of the first seventh arpeggio I teach in *Sweep Picking Speed Strategies for Guitar*.

Major Extensions

As with major seventh chords, major ninths (1, 3, 5, 7, 9) can be used as I or IV chords in a major key. To convert a major 7th arpeggio into a major 9th, the root notes on the 4th and 1st strings are raised by a tone.

Cmaj7 (I or IV)   Cmaj9 (I or IV)

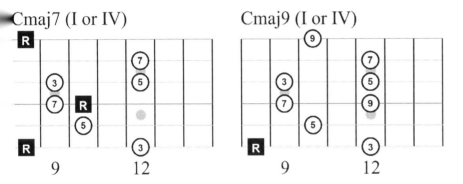

For all the pinky-finger haters out there, I have a position-shifting alternative for you! My picking and fingering preferences for Cmaj7 and the two versions of Cmaj9 are noted in Example 5a.

Cmaj9 sliding (I or IV)

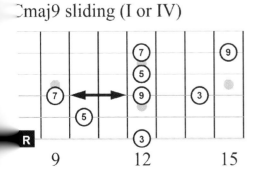

Example 5a:

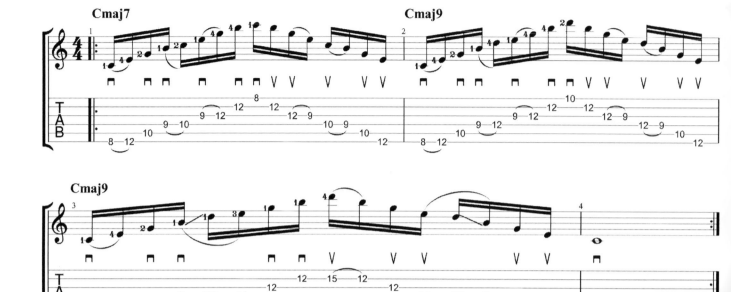

Major eleventh chords (1, 3, 5, 7, 9, 11) are avoided because of the semitone clash between the 3rd and 11th, and a tritone is created between the 7th and 11th. That's nerd-talk for *it sounds pretty bad.*

However, a #11 sound is perfect if you want to create a Lydian tonality.

The full chord symbol for an 11th chord built on the IV degree of the scale is maj9#11, constructed 1, 3, 5 7, 9, #11. To fit the #11 note into the arpeggio form, I replace the 3rd degree on the G string with the #11 two frets higher, then relocate the 5th degree from the G string to the B string. The latter move is just for fingering convenience, but also recreates the triad stacking layout that we saw back in Example 2n.

Since the arpeggio has grown, we must now use four strings to create the sound before any note repetition occur.

Cmaj9#11 (IV only)

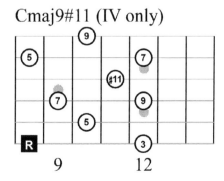

Example 5b:

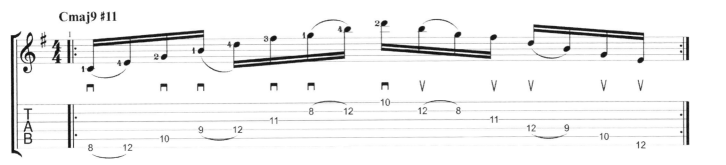

Major 13th chords do exist, but are handled differently for the I and IV chords. For the I chord (1, 3, 5, 7, 9, 11, 13), the 11th is omitted. A chord symbol like maj9(13) might be accurate, but it's common to see it noted as a 13th chord with an assumption that the 11th is omitted.

Shapes excluding the 11th can be used for I or IV chords, but an option exclusive to the IV chord (1, 3, 5, 7, 9, #11, 13) includes the raised 11th. To fit the 13th degree into either shape, I remove the redundant 5th and 7th degrees from the B string and place the 13th there instead. We are now using every scale note in one arpeggio!

Cmaj13 (I or IV)   Cmaj13#11 (IV only)

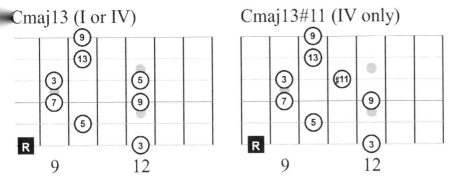

Example 5c:

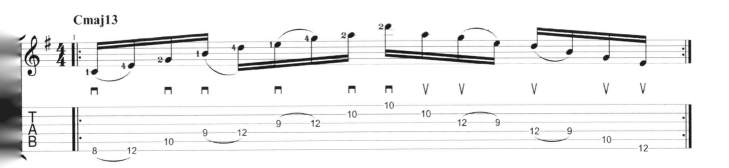

Example 5d:

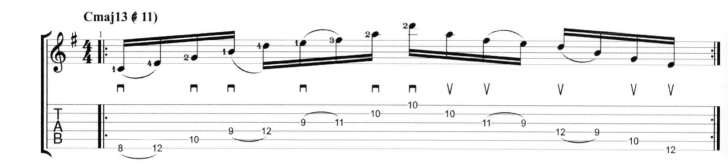

Dominant Extensions

Now that we have a process for building every extension from seventh arpeggios, working with dominant chords is easy, and there are only a few exceptions.

The transition from dominant seventh (1, 3, 5, b7) to dominant ninth (1, 3, 5, b7, 9) is the same as the major counterparts – you simply raise the root note by a tone to access the 9th.

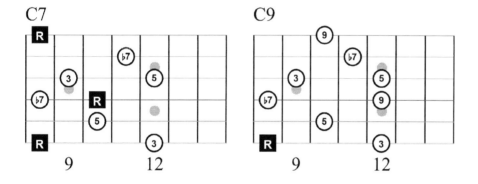

Since the shapes are straightforward, let's have a little more fun with the running order of the notes in Example 5e (C7) and Example 5f (C9).

Example 5e:

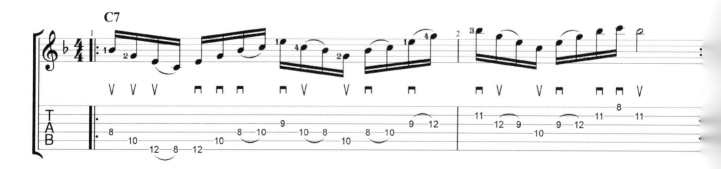

Example 5f:

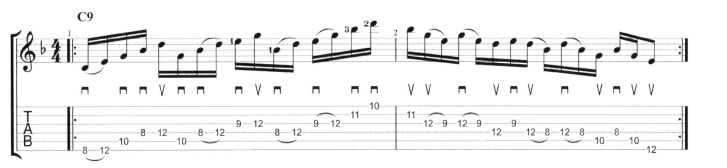

The use of unaltered dominant eleventh chords (1, 3, 5, b7, 9, 11) is a cause of some debate. There's no longer a tritone between the 7th and 11th, but the latter once again clashes with the 3rd. The dissonance can be lessened by making sure the 11th is as far away from the 3rd as possible, but it's still a sound that many find unpleasant.

To add to the confusion, some players will use chord symbols like C11 (C, E, G, Bb, D, F) to describe a *slash chord* like Bb/C (C, Bb, D, F), or a suspended chord like C9sus4 (C, F, G, Bb, D) – neither of which contain E notes (the 3rd of C).

From an arpeggio-playing point of view, my solution is to either arpeggiate it in a way that includes the 3rd and 11th in different octaves, or replace the 3rd in both octaves to create more of a suspended sound. The choice is yours, depending on the voicing of the chord underneath.

In this example with a C root note, I've replaced the E on the 12th fret of the low E string with an F (which can be played on the 8th fret of the A string). To bring the 3rd back into play, simply lower the first F note back to an E. You can also make this modification to Example 5g, which features an F note on the 13th fret of the low E string.

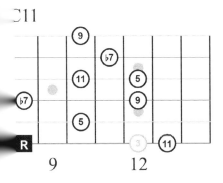

Example 5g:

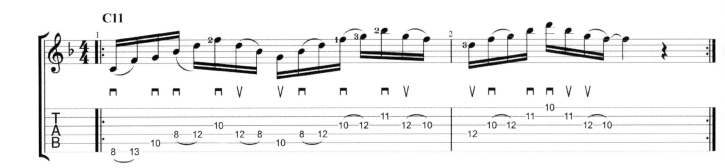

As with the major 13th arpeggio, a dominant 13th arpeggio omits the 11th and reinstates the 3rd. To bridge the intervallic gap between the 9th and 13th degrees, I repeat the 3rd and 5th degrees on the G string.

C13

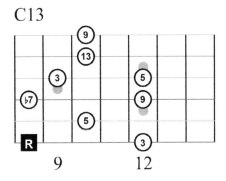

Example 5h:

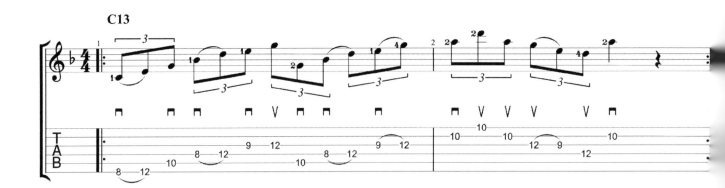

As with all arpeggios, it's essential to consult the voicing of the underlying chord to avoid clashes.

Minor Extensions

Extended minor arpeggios don't have any avoid notes, but it's important to know how they are applied. Here's a summary of where they fit diatonically.

- Minor seventh arpeggios can be used over the II, III or VI chords

- Minor ninth arpeggios can be used over II or VI chords (chord III chord produces a flat 9th)

- Minor eleventh arpeggios can be used over II and VI chords

- From the III degree, a min7(11) arpeggio works as a substitute since it omits the 9th degree

- Minor thirteenth chords are specifically II chords because chord II is the only minor chord that contains a major 13th

Once you've covered the essential notes of an arpeggio, you can complete the rest of the shapes with whatever chord tones you'd like to repeat, so long as you don't overdo the upper extensions at the expense of the core chord quality.

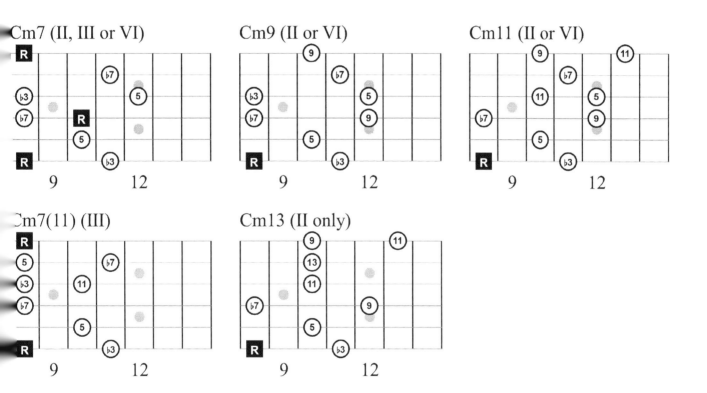

Once you've played the patterns a few times, jump into some licks!

Example 5i zig-zags through the minor seventh arpeggio with a mix of sweep picking and legato. Doubling back between the D and G strings is something I do a lot in arpeggio playing to break out of going straight up and down.

Example 5i:

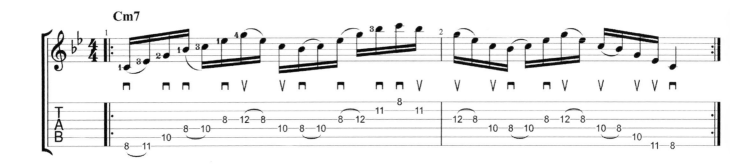

Example 5j once again emphasises the middle register and applies some doubling on the G and D strings in bar one of the Cm9 arpeggio.

Example 5j:

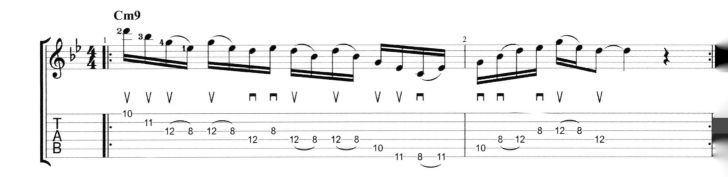

In Chapter Three, we used sequences and permutations to create interest. One of my favourite ways to creat even more attention is to use fives instead.

In Example 5k, bar one begins with five descending notes from the 11th degree, followed by another descendin five notes from the b7th degree on the B string. From there, two units of descending fours cross the bar lin before ascending from the low E string to the G string.

Example 5k:

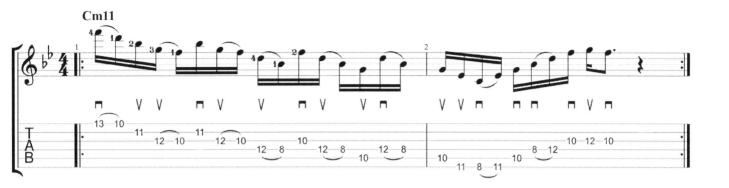

Example 5l cascades down the Phrygian-friendly alternative to m11 arpeggios. If playing this has the feel of a pentatonic scale, it's because C Minor pentatonic contains all the same notes. To preserve an arpeggio-sounding format, the F note on the A string and the C note on the D string in C Minor pentatonic have been omitted, since they are represented elsewhere within the lick.

Example 5l:

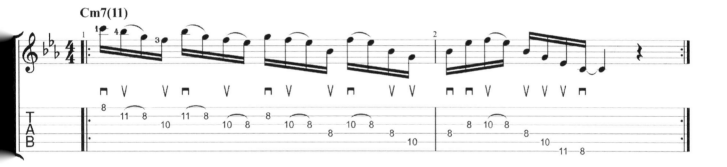

The Cm13 pattern in Example 5m uses 1/8th note triplets that start on the second-lowest string and end on the second-highest. Finishing on the A note emphasises that this is a m13 arpeggio.

All of the extended minor arpeggios work over simple triads. In this example, remember that the highest extension is suited to Dorian or II chord usage because of the natural 13th.

Example 5m:

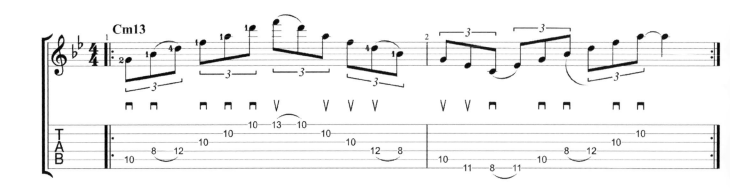

Diminished Extensions

The half-diminished (or m7b5) arpeggio is the most common extension of the triad built on the VII degree of the scale. A 9th chord is not viable, due to the dissonance that the minor 9th degree creates against the root note.

An option for extending beyond the 7th of the chord is to add the 11th degree, to create a m7b5(11). This chord has an even more mysterious sound than conventional diminished arpeggios thanks to the suspended sound of the 11th. To include the 11th degree, I rearrange the G and B strings.

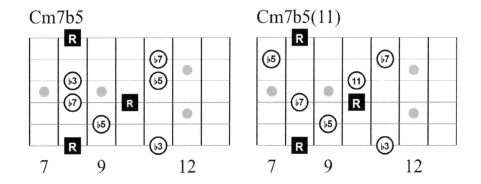

Example 5n:

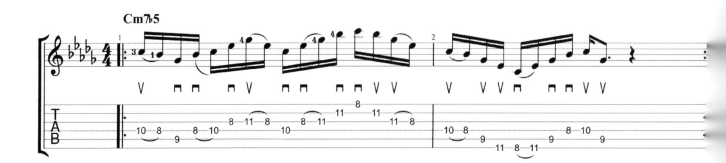

Playing the diminished 5th (an octave higher) right after the 11th creates an exotic sound, especially since the following interval (b7th) is a major 3rd interval higher.

Example 5o:

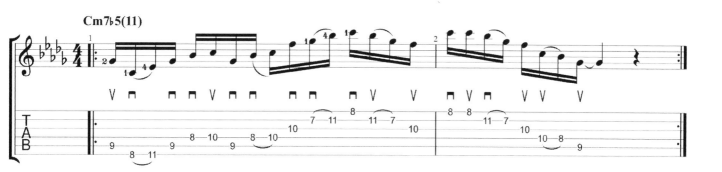

A full diminished seventh arpeggio (1, b3, b5, bb7) is comprised of constant minor 3rd intervals and fits in well with Harmonic Minor harmony. It is a symmetrical arpeggio than can be moved up and down in three-fret leaps to produce identically fingered inversions. It can be used wherever the diminished scale (a symmetrical scale comprised of alternating whole tones and semitones) is used.

To apply diminished seventh arpeggios to harmonic minor harmony, play them over the V chord by starting on the 3rd of the chord, then moving up or down in minor 3rd increments.

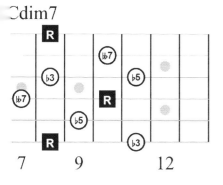

Example 5p:

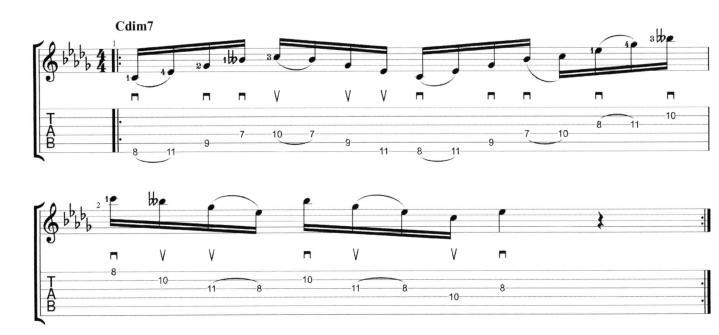

Now that you have the extended arpeggio shapes, let's use them as frameworks for some new arpeggio and scale combinations. The next four examples are in the key of G Major.

Example 5q uses the dominant ninth arpeggio shape and the fifth 3nps scale pattern of G Major. Beginning with a descending fours sequence, the lick moves through the arpeggio in bar one, beats 3 and 4 before a new scale fragment occurs in bar two. To remain within the frame of the arpeggio, scale notes on the B and high E strings draw from the fourth scale pattern.

Example 5q:

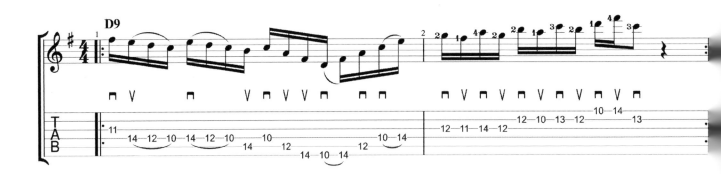

Using the major ninth arpeggio shape over the I chord in G Major, Example 5r recalls the sliding arpeggio shape from Example 5a. To blend the shape with notes of the scale, the lick uses notes from patterns one and two of the major scale. In bar one, beat 3, the slide into the 7th fret is just a stylistic choice which you'll hear in the audio.

Example 5r:

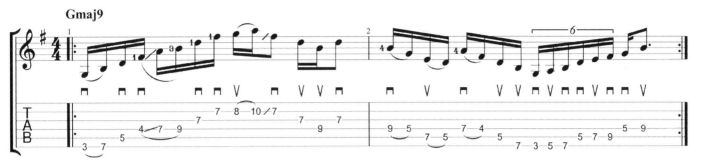

Example 5s is mostly a scalar lick but creates the sound of a minor thirteenth arpeggio with the fragments found at bar one, beat 4 and bar two, beats 1 and 4. Remember that you can use this lick over any II minor chord. You don't need permission to use the upper extensions!

Example 5s:

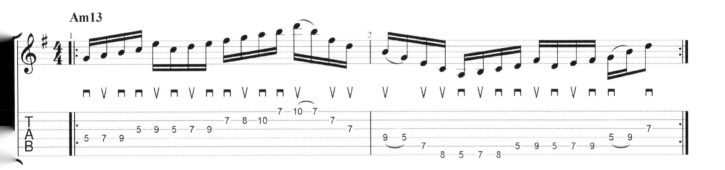

Finally, Example 5t extends beyond the underlying chord by implying a maj13#11 arpeggio over a Cmaj7 chord. Based on the fourth major scale pattern, this Lydian lick incorporates the arpeggio in bar one, beats 1 and 4. Pay close attention to the rhythmic notation, as the phrasing style of the lick incorporates several subdivisions.

Example 5t:

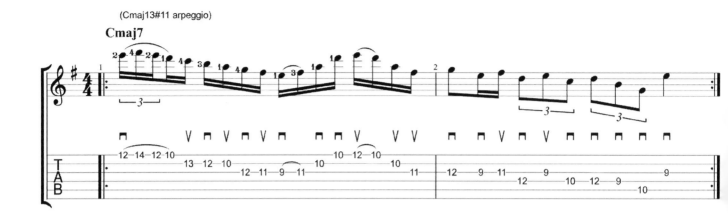

Extended Arpeggio Application: Key of G Major

Here is how the extended arpeggios fit into major scale harmony. Consider each row of this table a *chord family* that is expandable and contractible. You can play any of the arpeggios listed on the right over the chord on the left. This shows you how to use upper extensions of arpeggios even when a more straightforward chord is played underneath. A chord like Cmaj13#11 would be hard to voice on a guitar, but can still be outlined by using the arpeggio over a Cmaj7 chord.

An eleventh chord from the dominant family is, as previously covered, the one that requires the most consideration in voicings.

Triad	7th	9th	11th	13th
G	Gmaj7	Gmaj9	--	Gmaj13
Am	Am7	Am9	Am11	Am13
Bm	Bm7	--	Bm7(11)	--
C	Cmaj7	Cmaj9	Cmaj9#11	Cmaj13#11
D	D7	D9	D11	D13
Em	Em7	Em9	Em11	--
F#dim	F#m7b5	--	F#m7b5(11)	--

Bonus tips:

• Ninth chords beginning on scale degrees I, II, IV and V can be converted to 6/9 chords by replacing the 7th with major 6ths. In G Major, the new chords will be G6/9, Am6/9, C6/9 and D6/9

• F#m7b5 played in first inversion (A, C, E, F#) is the same as Am6 and can be used as a II chord.

• Altered dominants show up often in Jazz, Funk and Fusion styles. To convert any of the dominant shapes in this chapter to altered dominants (e.g., 7#5, 7#9, 7b9, 7b5b9 etc.) merely move the 5th or 9th degree up or down a semitone as required.

Chapter Homework: Extensions and Alterations

- Learn the shapes in this chapter from a single root note, paying attention to the intervals played

- Using the extended arpeggio table, play the arpeggios in each row

- Using the extended arpeggio table, play the arpeggios in each column

- Apply the examples from this chapter to improvisation applying sequences and scale integration

- Understand how each chord family can be extended with arpeggios

- Remember how to detour from avoid notes using the strategies in this chapter

Bonus Material: Chord Shapes

To give you some rhythm guitar options for your own jam tracks, here are some chord shapes, grouped into major, dominant, minor and diminished categories.

Major Chord Family:

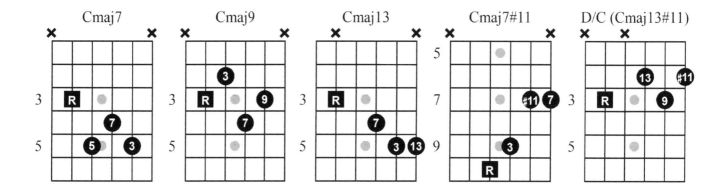

Dominant Chord Family:

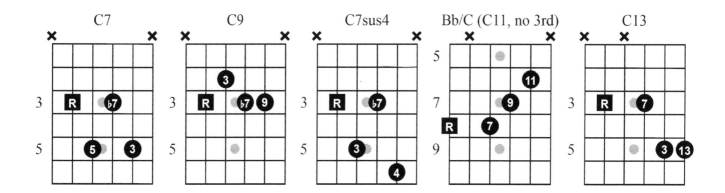

Minor Chord Family:

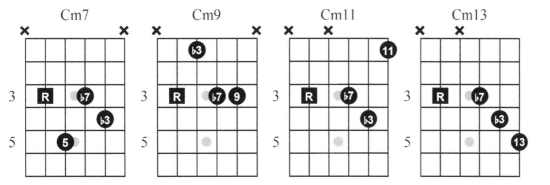

Diminished Chord Family:

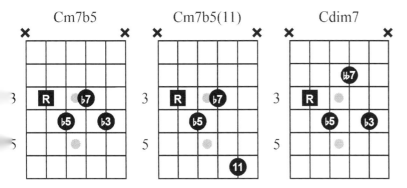

Chapter Six: Amaze While You Phrase

This chapter aims to guide you through ways of incorporating the content taught in previous chapters into your solos to create musical interest and personal phrasing when improvising. Rhythm, dynamics and articulation are just a few of the elements of music that make phrases sound like expression rather than exercises.

Creating Rhythmic Interest

Music is often compared to language, because done correctly, it delivers a clear message to the listener. Communicating verbally involves piecing together vocabulary, which is punctuated so that it can be understood, and then performed with a tone that conveys your message. As musicians, our aim should be to do the same on our instrument.

Many of the drills and licks in this book have been notated with streams of 1/16th notes or 1/8th note triplets. To help you develop some new rhythmic vocabulary, the next set of examples will emphasise variations using different note groupings, rests and *syncopation*. Syncopation is when a player deviates from an expected rhythm by emphasising weaker beats.

Using a base phrase (Example 6a), let's start with a series of descending fours using triad stacks (Bm, D, Em) over a Cmaj7 chord.

Example 6a:

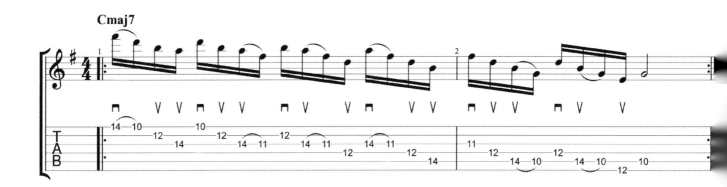

Now, there's nothing wrong with a bar of descending fours in 1/16th notes, but after that it gets a bit tedious because the listener hears where the line is going.

By just extending the duration of certain notes, we can use the same picking mechanics to create interest in the phrase before whipping out the barrage of 1/16ths.

Example 6b uses dotted 1/8th notes to begin the first three units of descending fours. This places melodic emphasis on the notes on beat one, the *and* of beat two, and on beat four. I like to accentuate these particular notes with extra pick attack.

Another great by-product of this change is that the consecutive 1/16th notes that follow in bar two are now a permutation of descending fours.

Example 6b:

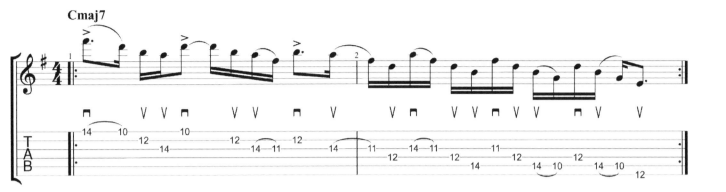

Example 6c again uses dotted 1/8ths to break up the phrase. Diverting from the convention in the middle of the phrase subverts expectations and sounds more musical than Example 6a.

Example 6c:

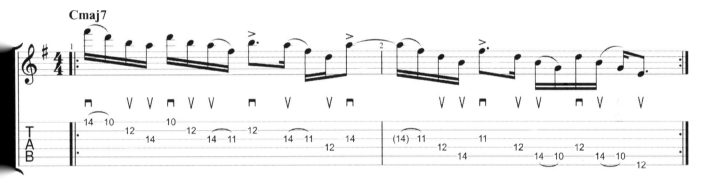

Next, let's retool a triad and scale combo used in Example 4h.

Example 6d:

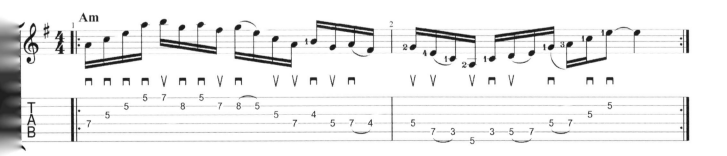

Four changes have been made to the lick in Example 6d to give it a different feel in Example 6e. The latter is a more Jazz Fusion-sounding phrase, reminiscent of Frank Gambale. The first four notes are played as 1/32nd notes and used as pickup notes for the main scalar phrase. Don't be put off by the speed since they just require a downward sweep of the pick.

In bar two, both B notes (7th fret, high E string; 4th fret, G string) have been lengthened, pushing back the scalar portions that follow each one. In bar three, beat 2, an 1/8th rest adds a small pause before the final ascent of the lick. The final phrase now begins on a downstroke.

Example 6e:

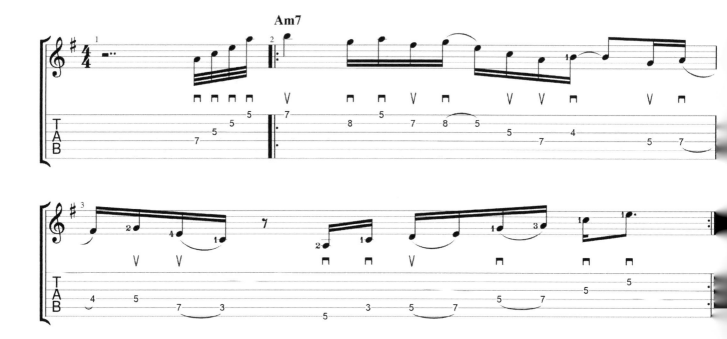

Let's rework one more example of scale and triad integration from Chapter Four. Compare the notation of Examples 6f and 6g.

Again, I've altered note durations and added rests to retool the phrasing of bar one. To accelerate the feel of the lick in bar two and fit in extra notes removed from the previous bar, beats 2 and 3 feature a legato burst of 1/16th triplets.

Example 6f:

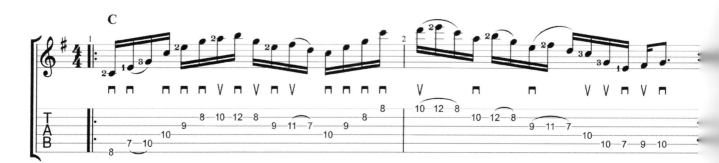

Example 6g:

Dynamics, Articulation and Control

As guitarists, we have many tools at our disposal for taking notes off the page and turning them into attention-grabbing phrases. Techniques like pick attack, slurs and palm muting help to create a wide dynamic range.

Example 6h moves down an A Minor seventh arpeggio, doubling the first two 1/16th notes of each beat. Try this with an even, moderate pick attack using your preferred picking system.

Example 6h:

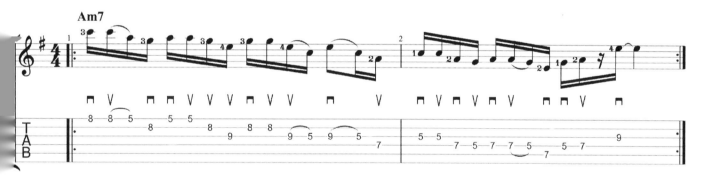

Use the playing directions noted in Example 6i to create a wide dynamic range within the lick. It now includes heavy-accented picked notes, pull-offs and palm muting. Exaggerate the accented pick strokes and palm mutes to hear the extreme difference in dynamics, then pull back a little to your own taste. Take a listen to the audio of both versions to experience the difference as a listener.

Example 6i:

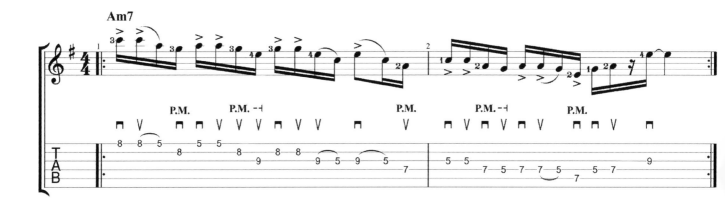

Sweep picking can join the party of palm muting and accented picking too. While it's nice to have smooth sweeps and consistent attack, it's even better to have options. Example 6j shows the way a common D Major triad is executed. Example 6k uses muted sweep picking to create a tight, staccato sound, contrasted by accenting the unmuted upstrokes.

Example 6j:

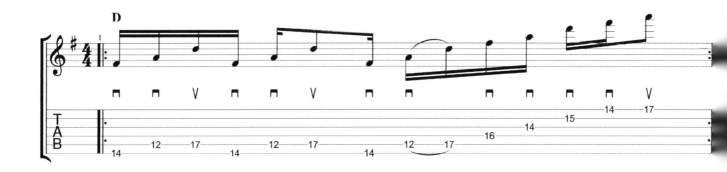

Example 6k:

Another tool for contrasted arpeggio playing is sweeping in one direction and using hammer-ons from nowhere in the other. Example 6l uses a regular ascending sweep followed by four hammered notes in the descent. In the tablature, these are marked as *left-hand taps*.

Bar two contains the same notes, but widens the dynamic range by using palm muting for the first four notes. For the legato portions of both bars (which I call *legarpeggios*), maintain clean execution by minimising noise from other strings as you hammer on.

Example 6l:

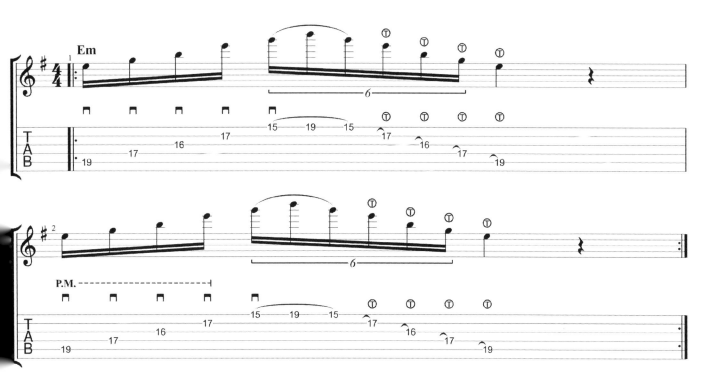

Adding taps from the picking hand in Example 6m extends the range of the legato portions of the arpeggio. Chances are, some of your favourite players are using fretting-hand legato in conjunction with sweep picking and tapping, not only for the smooth sound but also for the technical advantage of not having to re-engage the pick between fast blurs of 1/16th triplets.

Example 6m:

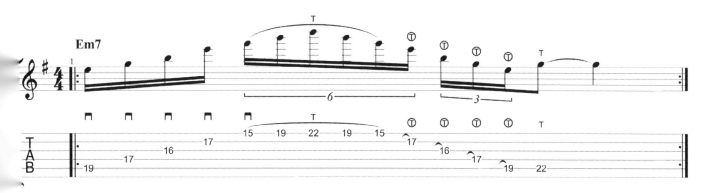

Melodic Mojo

It's important to remember that arpeggios are one of the ultimate melodic tools in improvisation. While commonly used in rock for the high-octane shred-a-thons, arpeggios are often the answer to the most common improvisation-related question: *How do I find the cool notes?*

The next examples are short solos with backing tracks that will help you hear how each melodic choice sits against the accompanying chord. Above each chord, I've written the melodic concept behind the notes.

The first solo (Example 6n) is to be played at a laid-back tempo of 70bpm, so don't be intimidated by the faster-looking runs. I've indicated suggested points for vibrato to really milk the longer notes.

Example 6n:

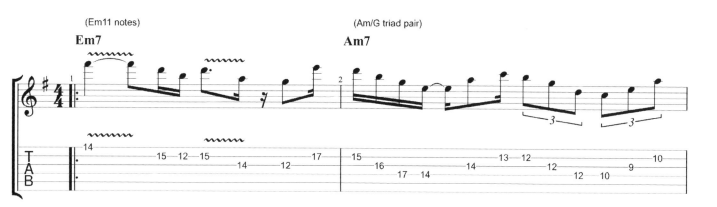

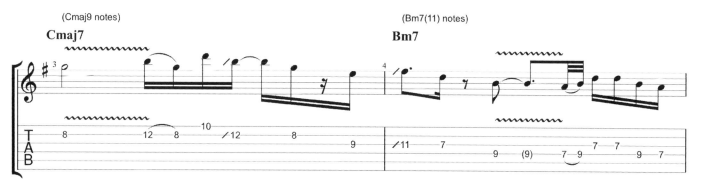

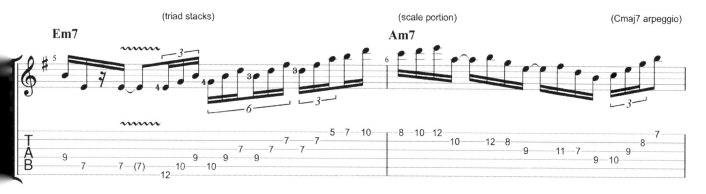

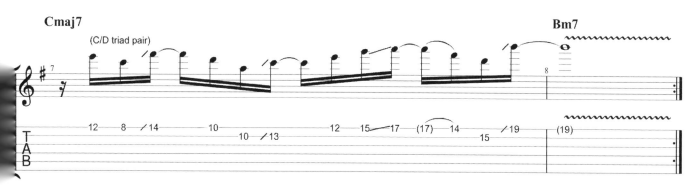

The second solo alternates between two keys using the D Mixolydian and C Mixolydian modes from the keys of G Major and F Major. Example 60 features groovy syncopated licks that use arpeggio fragments and triad pairs, concluding with a C Mixolydian scale run and sweep picking triad pairs. The pick stroke choices are optional for the first six bars, so go with whatever comes naturally. For the sake of completion, the tab includes all of my chosen pick strokes, accents and mutes.

Example 60:

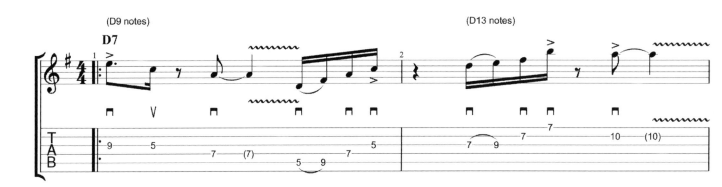

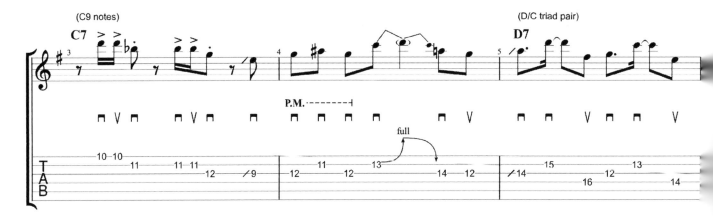

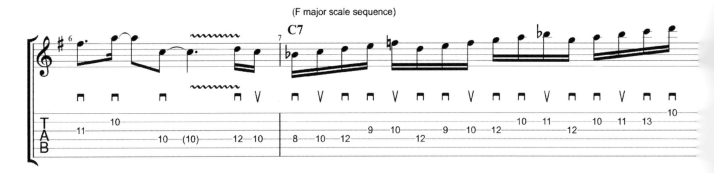

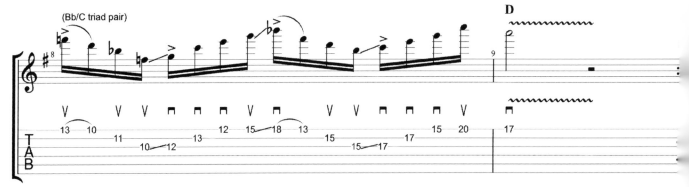

The final solo is an even mix of 1/8th note phrasing and faster ideas, showing no signs of the disconnect between shred and melody that many of us have experienced as players. As you can see from the rhythmic notation, bar four connects the two halves of the solo by mimicking the note placement of bar one before exploring some variations. I hope you dig this one because I had a lot of fun putting it together!

Example 6p:

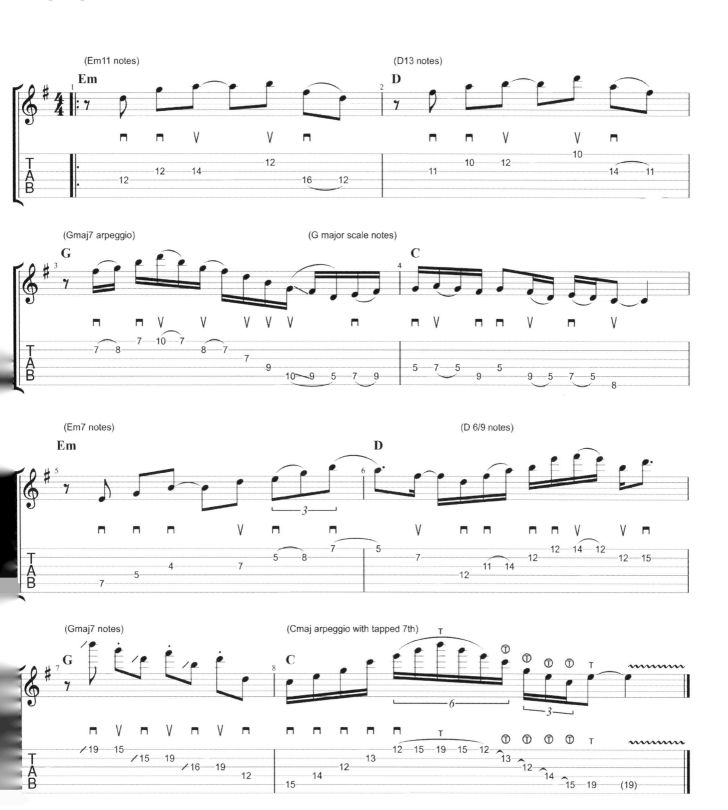

Chapter Homework: Phrasing and Articulation

- Select phrases from throughout the book that have relatively consistent note values

- Increase and decrease the note values at various points in each lick and use rests to emphasise different downbeats and upbeats of the bar

- Apply palm muting, accented picking or legato to increase the dynamic range

- Consult the feel of any rhythm tracks you jam over and punctuate your phrases in a way that gels with the musical surroundings

- Keep a mental catalogue of the rhythms you enjoy using in phrasing and try to use them in improvisation with different notes each time

Conclusion

You've completed your first read-through of the book, so now it's time to work towards internalising the material and applying your favourite concepts to actual music.

When you re-read and delve deeper into the mechanical, theoretical and musical ideas in these chapters, try to keep in mind that many players developed these approaches over decades, slowly and incrementally expanding their arpeggio-soloing vocabulary and phrasing skills from zero to hero. There's no pressure to master everything in the first reading because the most valuable information will take time to sink in!

We all have different styles and influences, so I suggest focusing on ideas that fit into the kind of music you enjoy, then develop as many variations and permutations as you can. Application is the key, so get jamming on these ideas!

Improvisation is the trial by fire of a musical statement, so when you hear a chord type, recall your options and execute the ideas you've mastered with purpose.

Happy music making!

Chris

Collect the Set!

Bestselling Titles from Chris Brooks

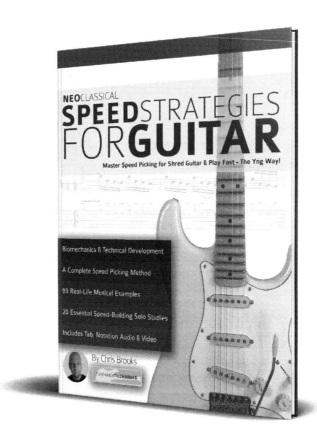

Neo-Classical Speed Strategies for Guitar

Master the Neo-Classical speed-picking system

- A definitive study of speed techniques and biomechanics for shred guitar

- A systematic guide to fast picking and string-change strategies

- Master the 9 principles of speed-picking as they're dissected, analysed and applied

- Complete technical development through over 90 real-life musical examples and "In the Style of" Licks

- 18 original Yngwie-inspired Neo-Classical studies to build guitar technique and consolidate every essential speed-picking principle

Neoclassical Speed Strategies for Guitar is the result of 27 years studying Neoclassical guitar, of one of the most influential pickers in guitar history. These principles will help you develop perfect guitar technique for any style.

You'll master picking biomechanics, technique, theory and hundreds of licks to turn you into a shred guitar monster.

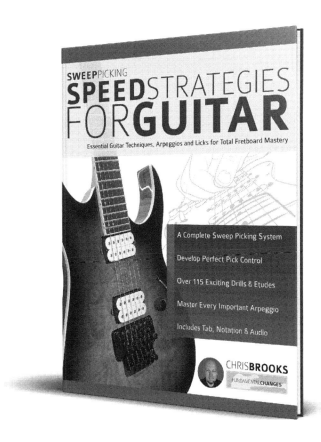

Sweep Picking Speed Strategies for Guitar

A Complete System to Master Sweep-picking on Guitar

A comprehensive breakdown of everything you need to sweep pick like a pro

A systematic guide to mastering technique and dominating the fretboard

Discover and apply the 6 Essential Rudiments of Sweep Picking

Complete technical development through 100 drills and 17 Etudes

Extensive library of arpeggio shapes and over 100 neck diagrams

Sweep Picking Speed Strategies for Guitar is the follow-up to Chris Brooks' wildly successful book Neoclassical Speed Strategies for Guitar. It takes a meticulous approach to breaking down the biomechanics of sweep picking and goes way beyond drills and guitar licks to get to the heart of great sweep picking technique.

You'll master everything from pick grip and fundamental rudiments to the execution of perfect, large-scale arpeggio forms for every common chord type as you learn sweep picking on guitar.

You'll become the sweep picking beast you never knew you could be!

Other Books from Fundamental Changes

The Complete Guide to Playing Blues Guitar Book One: Rhythm Guitar

The Complete Guide to Playing Blues Guitar Book Two: Melodic Phrasing

The Complete Guide to Playing Blues Guitar Book Three: Beyond Pentatonics

The Complete Guide to Playing Blues Guitar Compilation

The CAGED System and 100 Licks for Blues Guitar

Minor ii V Mastery for Jazz Guitar

Jazz Blues Soloing for Guitar

Guitar Scales in Context

Guitar Chords in Context

The First 100 Chords for Guitar

Jazz Guitar Chord Mastery

Complete Technique for Modern Guitar

Funk Guitar Mastery

The Complete Technique, Theory & Scales Compilation for Guitar

Sight Reading Mastery for Guitar

Rock Guitar Un-CAGED

The Practical Guide to Modern Music Theory for Guitarists

Beginner's Guitar Lessons: The Essential Guide

Chord Tone Soloing for Jazz Guitar

Chord Tone Soloing for Bass Guitar

Voice Leading Jazz Guitar

Guitar Fretboard Fluency

The Circle of Fifths for Guitarists

First Chord Progressions for Guitar

The First 100 Jazz Chords for Guitar

100 Country Licks for Guitar

Pop & Rock Ukulele Strumming

Walking Bass for Jazz and Blues

Guitar Finger Gym

The Melodic Minor Cookbook

The Chicago Blues Guitar Method

Heavy Metal Rhythm Guitar

Heavy Metal Lead Guitar

Progressive Metal Guitar

Heavy Metal Guitar Bible

Exotic Pentatonic Soloing for Guitar

The Complete Jazz Guitar Soloing Compilation

The Jazz Guitar Chords Compilation

Fingerstyle Blues Guitar

The Complete DADGAD Guitar Method

Country Guitar for Beginners

Beginner Lead Guitar Method

The Country Fingerstyle Guitar Method

Beyond Rhythm Guitar

Rock Rhythm Guitar Playing

Fundamental Changes in Jazz Guitar

Neo-Classical Speed Strategies for Guitar

100 Classic Rock Licks for Guitar

The Beginner's Guitar Method Compilation

100 Classic Blues Licks for Guitar

The Country Guitar Method Compilation

Country Guitar Soloing Techniques

Made in the USA
Middletown, DE
10 July 2019